Prayer Services for Parishes

KAREN BERRY, O.S.F.

ST. ANTHONY MESSENGER PRESS

Cincinnati, Ohio

Scripture passages have been taken from *New Revised Standard Version Bible,* copyright ©1989 by the Division of Christian Education of the National Council of the Churches of Christ in the U.S.A., and used by permission. All rights reserved.

Book design by Sandy L. Digman
Cover design by Mark Sullivan

Library of Congress Cataloging-in-Publication Data

Berry, Karen, 1943-
  Prayer services for parishes / Karen Berry.
    p. cm.
  ISBN 0-86716-586-3 (pbk. : alk. paper) 1. Catholic
Church—Liturgy—Texts. 2. Occasional
services—Catholic Church. I. Title.

BX1981.A2 2005
264'.0272-dc22

2005016201

ISBN 0-86716-586-3

Published by St. Anthony Messenger Press.
28 W. Liberty St.
Cincinnati, OH 45202
www.AmericanCatholic.org

Printed in the United States of America.
Printed on acid-free paper.

05 06 07 08 09 5 4 3 2 1

Contents

Dedication

To my mother, Lucille,
who taught me to pray
and who nurtured my faith
during all my growing-up years.

Introduction

This book is designed to be a resource for parishes. It provides prayer services for all kinds of occasions, seasons and programs. The content is purposely structured as "seven times seven" (seven topic areas with seven prayer services for each topic). The biblical significance of the number seven is profound. It indicates completion, perfection, fullness. For example, the first creation story in the book of Genesis uses a seven-day pattern, and Jesus taught his followers to forgive seventy times seven times.

These forty-nine prayers are by no means perfectly complete for all the needs a parish has. But they symbolize the fullness of turning to God on any and all occasions. Each service can be expanded, as needed, through the creative ideas of parish staffs. Each prayer provides a springboard for opening people to the action of God in the church community. Each set of prayers could spark ideas for other prayer topics.

As this resource is used in a faith community throughout the year, may the blessings of God be poured out—on the people, on the work, on the outreach. May those who pray be touched by the awareness that all is holy, and may the prayers extend far beyond the group who gathers to speak them.

(Note: Hymns for each prayer service are only suggestions. Other hymns, appropriate to the themes, can be substituted. All hymns offered here for opening and closing songs are located in either the *Breaking Bread* hymnal or the *Spirit and Song* book from OCP Publications in Portland, Oregon. The meditation songs by Liam Lawton, suggested for quiet reflection in several of the prayer services, are on his CD titled *In the Quiet* from GIA Publications in Chicago, Illinois.)

PART I

✠

Prayer Services
for the Liturgical Year

Prayer During Advent

Suggestion for atmosphere: Use an Advent wreath and symbols for each "O Antiphon." Symbols are suggested below.

Light the Advent wreath while the opening song is sung.

Opening Song: "Maranatha" by G. Westphal (K & R Music)

Opening Prayer: Advent is a time of longing. We experience the darkness in our world, and we hope for a better tomorrow. We long for the Lord of Love to come to heal our broken world. Wisdom in our lives tells us that to make room for the healing, we must act in loving ways. Saint Paul gives us this reminder in his letter to the Romans.

Reader 1: Romans 13:8–12

Response: Psalm 27:1, 3–8, 11, 13–14

Side 1: The LORD is my light and my salvation;
    whom shall I fear?
The LORD is the stronghold of my life;
    of whom shall I be afraid?
All: Be strong, and let your heart take courage;
    wait for the Lord!

Side 2: Though an army encamp against me,
    my heart shall not fear;
Though war rise up against me,
    yet I will be confident.
All: Be strong, and let your heart take courage;
    wait for the Lord!

Side 1: One thing I ask of the LORD,
    that will I seek after:
to live in the house of the LORD
    all the days of my life,
to behold the beauty of the LORD,
    and to inquire in his temple.
All: Be strong, and let your heart take courage;
    wait for the Lord!

Side 2: For he will hide me in his shelter
    in the day of trouble;
he will conceal me under the cover of his tent;
    he will set me high on a rock.
All: Be strong, and let your heart take courage;
    wait for the Lord!

Side 1: Now my head is lifted up
    above my enemies all around me,
and I will offer in his tent
    sacrifices with shouts of joy;
    I will sing and make melody to the LORD.
All: Be strong, and let your heart take courage;
    wait for the Lord!

Side 2: Hear, O LORD, when I cry aloud,
    be gracious to me and answer me!
All: Be strong, and let your heart take courage;
    wait for the Lord!

Side 1: "Come," my heart says, "seek his face!"
    Your face, LORD, do I seek.
All: Be strong, and let your heart take courage;
    wait for the Lord!

Side 2: Teach me your way, O LORD,
    and lead me on a level path
    because of my enemies.
All: Be strong, and let your heart take courage;
    wait for the Lord!

Side 1: I believe that I shall see the goodness of
    the LORD
    in the land of the living.
All: Be strong, and let your heart take courage;
    wait for the Lord!

Leader: When the prophet Isaiah prepared the people for the coming of God in glory, he compared the tenderness of God to the caring actions of a shepherd for his lambs.

Reader 2: Isaiah 40:3–5, 9–11

Leader: Let us sing our response to this reading.

Song: "Every Valley" by Bob Dufford, S.J. (OCP)

Leader: There is a beautiful Advent tradition that has become the "countdown" to Christmas. It is a series of prayers called the "O Antiphons," used one-by-one from December 17 to December 23. Each antiphon gives a title to Jesus, based on an Old Testament image. The prayer then calls upon Jesus to come and be the fulfillment of those Old Testament expectations. Tonight we will pray all of those Antiphons. For each one, a symbol will be brought forward and placed around the Advent wreath.

Reader 1: To call Jesus *Wisdom* is to place him in the presence of the Creator from the beginning of time. It is to acknowledge him as the Word of God, the greatest communication from our Covenant God who wants to be in relationship with us.

Symbol: Bible

All: O Wisdom, of our God Most High, guiding creation with power and love: teach us to walk in the paths of knowledge!

Reader 2: To call Jesus *Adonai* is to proclaim him Lord and one with God. It is to identify him with the mysterious "I Am" who encountered Moses in a burning bush and sent him to liberate people from oppression and bind them to a covenant of love.

Symbol: representation of burning bush, tablets of the law

All: O Adonai, Leader of ancient Israel, giver of the law to Moses on Sinai: rescue us with your mighty power!

Reader 1: To call Jesus the *Flower of Jesse* is to link Jesus with the family tree of David, son of Jesse. It is to show that the coming of Jesus brings the full flowering of the messianic promise that a savior of the people would be born from David's family line.

Symbol: flower, family tree

All: O Flower of Jesse's stem, sign of God's love for all people: save us without delay!

Reader 2: To call Jesus the *Key of David* is to unlock the mystery of God's promise to David that his kingdom would last forever. It is to declare that Jesus' teaching about the spiritual nature of God's kingdom clarifies any mistaken ideas that temporal kingdoms will have no end.

Symbol: large key

All: O Key of David, opening the gates of God's eternal Kingdom: free the prisoners of darkness!

Reader 1: To call Jesus *Radiant Dawn* is to herald a new beginning with his coming. It is to see the sun rising on an era of justice, love and kindness.

Symbol: picture of sunrise

All: O Radiant Dawn, splendor of eternal light, sun of justice: shine on those lost in the darkness of death!

Reader 2: To call Jesus *King of All Nations* is to erase the geographical boundaries normally associated with kingdoms. It is to focus on Jesus as a unifying leader who brings all people of the world together.

Symbol: globe, crown

All: O King of all nations, source of your church's unity and faith: save us all, your own creation!

Reader 1: To call Jesus *Emmanuel* is to recognize that in and through Jesus, God is present to us. It is to celebrate the even greater fulfillment of Isaiah's prophecy to the people of Judah that God would be present to them through the fidelity of a good king.

Symbol: manger with crown

All: O Emmanuel, God's presence among us, our King, our Judge: save us, Lord our God!

Leader: As we go forth to continue our prayerful preparation for Christmas, may we hold in our hearts the rich symbols of God's presence and love which we have been reminded of today. May our longing for the coming of Jesus fill us with hope and joy.

Closing Song: "Let the Valleys Be Raised" by Dan Schutte (OCP)

Prayer at Christmas Time

Suggestion for atmosphere: a Christmas tree or wreath and a nativity scene.

Opening Song: "Rise Up, Shepherd, and Follow" (African American Spiritual)

Opening Prayer: God, we celebrate your gift of Jesus, Savior of our world; your gift of Mary, willing mother of the Redeemer; your gift of Joseph, strong protector of mother and child; your gift of shepherds, witnesses of the miracle of Christmas; your gift of angels, heralds of glad tidings; your gift of creatures great and small, acknowledging the Creator. Our hearts are full of joy and gratitude. We celebrate you!

Reader: Luke 2:8–14

Response: "Angels We Have Heard on High" (traditional French carol)

Leader: Christmas is variously described as magical, mysterious, wondrous, joyful, peaceful. It conjures up nostalgic memories of childhood wonder, tastes and smells unique to the season, warm family ties and special romantic moments.

But Christmas has also become associated with frantic shopping days, cards to write, gifts to give or not to give, recipes and guest lists, decorating, winter colds and flu and holiday exhaustion.

Wherein lies the real Christmas? An attempt to enter into the reality of Mary and Joseph's experience could help us find it. The location is Bethlehem and the time is during the reign of Caesar Augustus in Rome, with Herod ruling Jerusalem. A very pregnant young woman and a very concerned husband have just arrived after a long, difficult journey through hills and valleys. There is nothing peaceful or welcoming about the noisy, over-crowded town. Stumbling through the dark, seeking shelter, feeling hungry, aware that the time for giving birth is drawing near, they gratefully accept the only accommodations available to them—a cave in the side of a hill outside the town.

And here is where the magic and the mystery, the wonder and joy occur. Our legends give us singing angels, a bright star and gifts from strangers because God came to live among us and that's a cause for miracles. The magic of that birth has a power to transcend time and to touch our hectic, frantic rush to Christmas in such a way that, despite all the craziness, we too come to a special moment. Finally, all is still and the mystery enfolds us in peaceful wonder. Christmas happens, ready or not, because God chooses to be with us.

Let us pause to reflect.

After reflection time, invite the group to share spontaneous stories of Christmas "miracles" or stories of how they found some peace and stillness in the midst of the hectic "Christmas rush."

PRAYER

Leader: For the gift of your love.
All: We thank you, God.

Leader: For the many ways you come to us.
All: We thank you, God.

Leader: For the people who are in our lives.
All: We thank you, God.

Leader: For the teachings of Jesus.
All: We thank you, God.

Leader: For the innocence of children.
All: We thank you, God.

Leader: For the sacrifices of parents.
All: We thank you, God.

Leader: For messengers of good news.
All: We thank you, God.

Leader: For the wonders of creation.
All: We thank you, God.

Pause for spontaneous prayers of gratitude.

CONCLUSION

Leader: With glad hearts we joyfully come to the manger to worship the child. And with glad hearts we run to share the news of God living among us and sharing our lives. May the wonder of Christmas renew us, Lord. May our faith make us strong, humble and childlike. We ask this in the name of Jesus, reborn again and again in our lives. Amen.

Closing Song: "Children, Run Joyfully" by Bob Dufford, s.j. (OCP)

Prayer During Ordinary Time

Suggestion for atmosphere: anything to create a joyful atmosphere, such as balloons, bells, cymbals, streamers, liturgical dancers.

Opening Song: "To You, O God, I Lift Up My Soul" by Bob Hurd (OCP)

Opening Prayer: It is good to celebrate the ordinary things in our lives, O God, because most of our days are ordinary and you are always there. We want to acknowledge that your presence makes our daily striving productive and your support makes our every effort blessed. We praise you for the ordinary days of our lives.

Reading: 2 Peter 1:3–8

Response: Psalm 25:1, 2, 4–10, 12–13, 20–21

Use the refrain from the opening song as a response to each verse, with dancers and streamers as an option.

Reader: O my God, in you I trust; do not let me be put to shame; do not let my enemies exult over me. Make me to know your ways, O Lord; teach me your paths. Lead me in your truth, and teach me, for you are the God of my salvation; for you I wait all day long.
All: To you, O God, I lift up my soul; lift up my spirit to my Lord. To you I lift up my soul.

Reader: Be mindful of your mercy, O Lord, and of your steadfast love, for they have been from of old. Do not remember the sins of my youth or my transgressions; according to your steadfast love remember me, for your goodness' sake, O Lord!
All: To you, O God, I lift up my soul; lift up my spirit to my Lord. To you I lift up my soul.

Reader: Good and upright is the Lord; therefore he instructs sinners in the way. He leads the humble in what is right, and teaches the humble his way. All the paths of the Lord are steadfast love and faithfulness, for those who keep his covenant and his decrees.
All: To you, O God, I lift up my soul; lift up my spirit to my Lord. To you I lift up my soul.

Reader: Who are they that fear the Lord? He will teach them the way that they should choose. They will abide in prosperity, and their children shall possess the land.
All: To you, O God, I lift up my soul; lift up my spirit to my Lord. To you I lift up my soul.

Reader: Guard my life and deliver me; do not let me be put to shame, for I take refuge in you. May integrity and uprightness preserve me, for I wait for you.
All: To you, O God, I lift up my soul; lift up my spirit to my Lord. To you I lift up my soul.

Reading: Ecclesiastes 3:1–15

LITANY

Leader: To you who blesses each new day with your Presence.
All: To you, O God, I lift up my soul.

Leader: To you who fills ordinary time with gracious gifts.
All: to you, O God, I lift up my soul.

Leader: To you who puts a song in the heart and a striving in the spirit.
All: To you, O God, I lift up my soul.

Leader: To you who directs thoughts, gathers feelings and guides actions.
All: To you, O God, I lift up my soul.

Leader: To you who imprints the seal of your love on all you create.
All: To you, O God, I lift up my soul.

Leader: To you who shares creative energy and quiet strength.
All: To you, O God, I lift up my soul.

Leader: To you who anoints each participant in your eternal plan.
All: To you, O God, I lift up my soul.

Leader: To you who affirms every honest effort and courageous step.
All: To you, O God, I lift up my soul.

Leader: To you who touches every movement and every outcome.
All: To you, O God, I lift up my soul.

Leader: To you who brings peace in the stillness of the night.
All: To you, O God, I lift up my soul.

Prayer: O God, who is always with us, move us to see beauty in the ordinary. It is your loving presence in the common stuff of life that makes our lives touchingly beautiful. We praise you for our physical and mental abilities we often take for granted. We thank you for the insights and the strength that move us along our daily journey. We humbly acknowledge that our limited vision cannot see your broader plan, but we believe that, in step with you, we can contribute our own small part. An extraordinary God fills our ordinary days, and for this our hearts sing your praises! Amen.

Closing Song: "Though the Mountains May Fall" by Dan Schutte (OCP)

Optional: liturgical dancing

Prayer During Lent

Suggestion for atmosphere: a table draped in purple cloth; on the table, a container of ashes (or pile of ashes), a Bible and a cross.

Opening Song: "Save Your People" by Jim Farrell (OCP)

Participants process in very slowly during the singing. The leader sprinkles them with ashes as they enter. Return unused ashes to the table.

Opening Prayer: Marked with the ashes of this Lenten season, we come before you in our sinfulness, Lord. Aware that without you we can do nothing, we offer our shortcomings in the hope that you will lead us to transformation.

Reading: Joel 1:13–14; 2:12–17

Response: Psalm 28:1–3, 7–9

Side 1: To you, O Lord, I call;
    my rock, do not refuse to hear me,
for if you are silent to me,
  I shall be like those who go down
    to the Pit.
All: Save your people, O Lord.

Side 2: Hear the voice of my supplication,
    as I cry to you for help,
as I lift up my hands
    toward your most holy sanctuary.
All: Save your people, O Lord.

Side 1: Do not drag me away with the wicked,
    with those who are workers of evil,
who speak peace with their neighbors,
    while mischief is in their hearts.
All: Save your people, O Lord.

Side 2: The LORD is my strength and my shield;
    in him my heart trusts;
so I am helped, and my heart exults,
    and with my song I give thanks to him.
All: Save your people, O Lord.

Side 1: The LORD is the strength of his people;
    he is the saving refuge of his anointed.
All: Save your people, O Lord.

Side 2: O save your people, and bless your heritage;
be their shepherd, and carry them forever.
All: Save your people, O Lord.

Reading: Jonah 3:1–10

Leader: Knowing that constant effort is required as we attempt to live our Christian commitments day by day, we approach you with bold confidence, Lord. We offer you the best we can give, knowing we will need your loving assistance to help us keep the pledges we dare to make. We honor the season of Lent and its call to renewal by offering these promises:

Leader: To act with justice in all our dealings.
All: This we pledge, O Lord.

Leader: To use only what we need and to live without excess.
All: This we pledge, O Lord.

Leader: To remember you and to honor you as we go through each day.
All: This we pledge, O Lord.

Leader: To love others unconditionally and selflessly.
All: This we pledge, O Lord.

Leader: To always be open to learning from others.
All: This we pledge, O Lord.

Leader: To be caretakers of all that is entrusted to us.
All: This we pledge, O Lord.

Leader: To be peacemakers in our communities, families and workplaces.
All: This we pledge, O Lord.

Leader: To respect and promote truth in words and actions.
All: This we pledge, O Lord.

Leader: To offer our time and our resources generously.
All: This we pledge, O Lord.

Leader: To be humble enough to receive as graciously as we give.
All: This we pledge, O Lord.

Leader: To respond with gentle understanding when things are not done as we think they should be done.
All: This we pledge, O Lord.

Leader: To live beyond fear, entrusting to you our belief that all will be well.
All: This we pledge, O Lord. Carrying these pledges in our hearts, we offer our good will upon the altar of our lives. Take the sacrifices of our good intentions, Lord, and transform them into deeds that will, in turn, change our lives. May we approach Easter unafraid of transformation and more open to being fully alive in you. Amen.

Closing Song: "Ashes" by Tom Conry (OCP)

Prayer in the Easter Season

Suggestion for atmosphere: Easter lilies, a cross draped in white cloth, paper and pencils for participants.

Opening Song: "Alleluia! Alleluia! Let the Holy Anthem Rise" (Anonymous)

Opening Prayer: To you, Risen Lord, we offer our tears turned to laughter, our pain turned to joy, our fear turned to glad confidence. Your victory over death puts hope in our hearts. Your disciples didn't lose you forever, nor have we lost those we love. By your Resurrection, you show us that life is eternal. We praise and bless you. Amen.

Reading: Luke 24:36–48

Response: Psalm 47

Side 1: Clap your hands, all you peoples;
   shout to God with loud songs of joy.
For the LORD, the Most High, is awesome,
   a great king over all the earth.
All: The Lord, the Most High, is awesome.

Side 2: He subdued peoples under us,
   and nations under our feet.
He chose our heritage for us,
   the pride of Jacob whom he loves.
All: The Lord, the Most High, is awesome.

Side 1: God has gone up with a shout,
   the LORD with the sound of a trumpet.
Sing praises to God, sing praises;
   sing praises to our King, sing praises.
All: The Lord, the Most High, is awesome.

Side 2: For God is the king of all the earth;
   sing praises with a psalm.
God is king over the nations;
   God sits on his holy throne.
All: The Lord, the Most High, is awesome.

Side 1: The princes of the peoples gather
   as the people of the God of Abraham.
For the shields of the earth belong to God;
   he is highly exalted.
All: The Lord, the Most High, is awesome.

Reading:

It is significant that the Risen Christ identified himself to troubled and doubting followers not by brilliant persuasion nor by miracles, but by his scars. It was his suffering, transformed by God, that made him credible. Likewise we, too, need not despair because of the scars that identify us. It is precisely these scars that God transforms into ultimate good for ourselves and compassionate ministry to others.

When the worst that life might deal us can be so transformed, we encounter a "resurrection psychology." Our confidence lies not in preventing anything bad from happening to us, nor in seeking perfect healing of our psychological wounds, but rather our confidence lies in the transforming power of God promised us through the Resurrection of Jesus Christ.[1]

Pause for silent reflection.

Leader: Margaret Alter, the author of the reading we just heard, said that God transforms our scars into "ultimate good for ourselves and compassionate ministry to others." On the paper you have received, list examples from your own life where you have found this to be true.

Pause for writing. After a suitable time has passed, invite participants to share whatever they feel comfortable sharing. Depending on the size of the group, this could be done in small groups or with the whole.

CLOSING PRAYER

All: Jesus, take our scars and transform them into something good. Take away any bitterness that may still be attached to our wounds. While we do not take joy in the pain that caused those scars, we do rejoice in the potential for growth and the direction for new life that those painful incidents from our past have given us. We believe that you rose to new life after all the pain inflicted on you. We believe we can rise too, with your help. Please show us the way. Amen.

Closing Song: "Alleluia! Alleluia!" (sung to "Ode to Joy," Beethoven)

Prayer at Pentecost

Suggestion for atmosphere: tongues of fire symbols and/or red candles; instrumental music for the guided imagery.

Opening Song: "Holy Spirit" (verses 1 and 2), by Ken Canedo (OCP)

Leader: Welcome to a celebration of the coming of the Spirit! Today we will look within to find the Spirit who is readily available to us. This was the promise of Jesus to his followers, as we hear in the Gospel.

Reader: John 14:15–21, 26

Leader: Believing these words of Jesus, let us now touch the truth that abides in us.

Instruct people to close their eyes, slow down their breathing and relax. Soft background music may be used throughout this guided meditation. Read slowly, and pause after each phrase.

GUIDED IMAGERY

Leader: You are in a semi-darkened room. A few candles are flickering a little distance away from you. Take a deep breath and set aside any tension you might have been feeling. There is peace in this place. As the peace envelops you, you begin to feel a Presence. This Presence surrounds you and you feel protected, loved and strengthened. Memories come to you of family and friends who ever nurtured, loved and supported you. All of them are somehow part of this gentle Presence. You invite this Presence to come closer.

You feel touched, not physically but in the deepest part of your spirit. This Presence has a familiar feel, as if it has always been with you.

But now it is stronger than ever before, burning like the flames from the candles. The burning doesn't sting; it warms and enlivens you. You feel a passion for living—a passion that makes every obstacle seem small.

Speak to this Presence about any challenges or difficulties you have been facing.

Observe a longer pause.

Listen for a response. Acknowledge that this Presence is the Spirit of God who loves you very much. Welcome the Holy Spirit to remain with you always. The room slowly grows lighter, and then brightens with an astounding warm radiance. Enjoy the bright warmth. When you are ready to bring that light with you, open your eyes.

Song: Use the opening song again, verses 3 and 4.

Reader: Isaiah 11:1–3a

Song: Use the opening song, verses 5 and 6

Leader: Holy Spirit, bringing us wisdom, we look to you for love and light and healing. Spirit of courage, we count on you to open doors and help us face tomorrow. Giver of gifts, teach us to value what is really important, to discern between options and to rest peacefully with our decisions. Fire the flame of love in us so we will reach out to others with the compassion you show to us.

All: Spirit of the Lord, rest on us with wisdom and understanding, with counsel and might, with knowledge and the fear of the Lord. Spirit of truth, abide in us. Amen.

Closing Song: *"Envia Tu Espiritu"* by Bob Hurd (OCP)

Prayer During the Time After Pentecost

Suggestion for atmosphere: Make eight signs proclaiming the highlights of the complete liturgical year:

> *Advent: Jesus Is Coming*
> *Christmas: Light and Peace*
> *Epiphany: A Star to Follow*
> *Lenten Journey: Sacrifice*
> *Holy Week: Jesus' Values*
> *Resurrection: Love Triumphs*
> *Holy Spirit: Sanctifier*
> *Christ Reigns: Loving Service*

Opening Song: "By the Waking of Our Hearts" by Ricky Manalo, C.S.P. (OCP)

Participants process with eight sign-bearers, who then take seats in the front row after entering.

Leader: Soon our liturgical year will have come full circle. Just as we assess our progress or recall our triumphs and failures when a calendar year comes to an end or when a new birthday approaches, so too can we use this time to reflect on where a church year has taken us.

After reading each description, pause for reflection. During the pause, the appropriate sign for that part of the liturgical year can be brought forward, with the sign-bearer facing the assembly and remaining in place until all signs are displayed. Optional: the refrain of the opening song can be sung by everyone at the end of each pause.

Reader: Recall the hope and joyful anticipation of the Advent season. To what did you give birth after waiting and longing?

Pause. Bring forward sign 1. Optional singing.

At Christmas we celebrated the Light coming into the world as our Prince of Peace. What darkness was dispelled for you and which obstacles to peace were removed?

Pause. Bring forward sign 2. Optional singing.

The post-Christmas days of child martyrs, wise men from the East and the Holy Family fleeing to safety mirrored the pain and effort of good people's daily quest to stay on the right path. Where did you find refuge or follow a star?

Pause. Bring forward sign 3. Optional singing.

When the season of Lent began, we were invited to renewal and sacrifice. How did you make your lenten journey an experience of reaching beyond yourself and seeing to other needs besides your own?

Pause. Bring forward sign 4. Optional singing.

On the holy days of our Christian year's holiest week, we walked with Jesus to the conclusion of his loving life. What did that teach you about life's greatest value and ultimate purpose?

Pause. Bring forward sign 5. Optional singing.

During the Easter season, we celebrated the mystery of life not ending, and we rejoiced that love really does triumph. When have you experienced the reality of that message?

Pause. Bring forward sign 6. Optional singing.

With the coming of the Spirit at Pentecost, we received the promise that Jesus remains uniquely with us. We celebrated that we are inspired and made holy by God who is always present to us. When have you felt that Presence, and how have you responded to the Spirit's urgings?

Pause. Bring forward sign 7. Optional singing.

Now we are in the season following Pentecost, and we move through each day aware of God's care. The liturgical year will end before Advent with a celebration of Christ as King. How are you living in these weeks of "ordinary time" to witness to Jesus' message of love, forgiveness and service?

Pause. Bring forward sign 8. Optional singing.

All signs remain displayed during this prayer:

Leader: Let us pray. In thanksgiving for whatever has been born in us during this past year.
All: We bless you, God, for Advent graces.

Leader: In gratitude for moments of light and opportunities to make peace.
All: We bless you, God, for Christmas graces.

Leader: In thanksgiving for assistance with our daily journey.
All: We bless you, God, for stars that guide us.

Leader: In gratitude for all that we have and are able to share.
All: We bless you, God, for the challenges of Lent.

Leader: In thanksgiving for giving our lives a noble purpose.
All: We bless you, God, for Jesus' life spent for us.

Leader: In gratitude for the power of love in our lives.
All: We bless you, God, for Easter graces.

Leader: In thanksgiving for your presence, your inspiration, and your prodding.
All: We bless you, God, for Pentecost graces.

Leader: In gratitude for teaching us to love, forgive and serve.
All: We bless you, God, for the graces of a liturgical year.

Leader: You have graced our year with everything we need, O God. The riches of your message and your presence astound us. How can we not be confident of your loving care when we see you everywhere! In every joy and in every sorrow we behold you accompanying us. In every choice and with every step we perceive you leading us. You are our strength and our hope. You know us and love us. We praise you, God!

Closing Song: "We Will Rise Again" by David Haas (OCP)

PART II

✠

Prayer Services
for Seasons and Holidays

A Prayer With Autumn Leaves

(to reflect on life's cycles)

Suggestion for atmosphere: *place brightly colored autumn leaves around a candle and Bible or, if the prayer is held outside, participants can gather around a tree that is dropping its leaves.*

Opening Song: "God's Love Is Everlasting" by Tom Tomaszek (OCP)

Opening Prayer: God of wonder and mystery, we gather here today (this evening) to celebrate the season of autumn and to reflect on its lessons. We believe that you speak to us through the world you have made, and so we turn in gratitude to the sights and sounds and smells of this season of change. We hold in reverence the last lingering bits of summer light. We watch in humble submission the signs of decay that so graphically remind us of our aging. We call on you to strengthen our faith when endings are imminent and new beginnings seem far away. Amen.

Reader: John 3:4–15

Response: Sirach 14:11–14, 17, 18

Side 1: My child, treat yourself well, according to your means,
    and present worthy offerings to the Lord.
Side 2: Remember that death does not tarry,
    and the decree of Hades has not been shown to you.

Side 1: Do good to friends before you die,
    and reach out and give to them as much as you can.
Side 2: Do not deprive yourself of a day's enjoyment;
    do not let your share of desired good pass by you.

Side 1: All living beings become old like a garment,
    for the decree from of old is, "You must die!"
Side 2: Like abundant leaves on a spreading tree that sheds some and puts forth others,
    so are the generations of flesh and blood:
    one dies and another is born.

Leader: Look around at the rich colors of autumn. Why is the prelude to death so spectacular? The deep green of summer is comforting and calming. It is ordinary and expected. It is the soft grass beneath our steps and the shady canopy overhead. It can be taken for granted, like the ordinary days of life following one upon another while we move along unaware of our own growing.

But the colors of autumn are startling. They say, "Wake up and see, because we won't last long." The yellows and reds will soon crunch beneath our feet as brown mulch for the earth. The brilliant leaves that draw our eyes upward will soon abandon their branches to stark loneliness and emptiness. Then we will look upon trees seeming to be dead while winter nurtures hidden energies and provides a womb for new life to emerge in the spring.

In this cycle there is a clue to the mystery of living and dying. The prelude to death is so spectacular because we must wake up and notice where life is taking us. We are growing and moving toward something that is not an end but a spectacular transformation.

All those we love, whose final moments are vested in unspeakable beauty, are showing us their entrance into mystery and their impetus to go on. Our own final moments will be colorful and energizing too. We will gather up all we have become in our march through ordinary days, and we will enter into a womb from which our new life will emerge.

During autumn we are watching a process of nature letting go. May we have the grace to allow autumn to be our teacher.

Let us pause to reflect.

Reader: Wisdom 7:15–22

Response: Psalm 136:1–9, 23–26

Side 1: O give thanks to the Lord, for he is good,
for his steadfast love endures forever.
Give thanks to the God of gods, for his
steadfast love endures forever.
Side 2: O give thanks to the Lord of lords, for his
steadfast love endures forever;
who alone does great wonders, for his
steadfast love endures forever.

Side 1: Who by understanding made the
heavens, for his steadfast love endures
forever;
who spread out the earth on the waters,
for his steadfast loves endures forever.
Side 2: Who made the great lights, for his
steadfast love endures forever;
the sun to rule over the day, for his steadfast
love endures forever;

Side 1: The moon and the stars to rule over the
night;
for his steadfast love endures forever
Side 2: It is he who remembered us in our low
estate, for his steadfast love endures
forever,
and rescued us from our foes, for his
steadfast love endures forever.

Side 1: Who gives food to all flesh, for his
steadfast love endures forever.
Side 2: O give thanks to the God of heaven, for
his steadfast love endures forever.

Prayer: God of wonder and mystery, you gave us
Jesus to go before us and to show us a way to
new life through our dying. As the season of
autumn reminds us that all living things must
die, so may our faith in the life Jesus promised
encourage us to embrace life's potential.
Rather than being saddened by life's endings,
may we find, in the wisdom of your creation,
the constantly renewing love that reassures us
of your presence. With our eyes on the tree of
life and its spectacular beauty, may we remain
always in Jesus. Amen.

Closing Song: "Now We Remain" by David Haas
(GIA)

A Prayer on Thanksgiving Day
(to remember and be grateful)

Suggestion for atmosphere: symbols of the
Thanksgiving holiday and of harvest time: cornucopia,
stalks of grain, pumpkins, colored leaves, various fruits.

Opening Song: "Come, Worship the Lord" by
John Michael Talbot (Birdwing Music and
BMG Songs, Inc./Cherry Lane Music
Publishing Co, Inc.)

Leader: Welcome to a celebration of thanksgiving.
Many times during the year we come to God
asking for things. This is good. God wants us
to express our needs and to trust that God will
provide. But today we come together to notice
how God has provided and to express exuber-
ant and abundant thanks for the bountiful
blessings.
Let us begin by reflecting on growth in the
kingdom of God.

Reader: Mark 4:26–29

Response: We praise you, God, for the harvest of
blessings!

PSALM 65:6–13

Side 1: By your strength you established the
mountains; you are girded with might. You
silence the roaring of the seas, the roaring of
their waves, the tumult of the peoples.
All: We praise you, God, for the harvest of
blessings!

Side 2: Those who live at earth's farthest bounds
are awed by your signs; you make the
gateways of the morning and the evening
shout for joy.

All: We praise you, God, for the harvest of blessings!

Side 1: You visit the earth and water it, you greatly enrich it; the river of God is full of water; you provide the people with grain, for so you have prepared it.
All: We praise you, God, for the harvest of blessings!

Side 2: You water its furrows abundantly, settling its ridges, softening it with showers, and blessing its growth.
All: We praise you, God, for the harvest of blessings!

Side 1: You crown the year with your bounty; your wagon tracks overflow with richness. The pastures of the wilderness overflow, the hills gird themselves with joy.
All: We praise you, God, for the harvest of blessings!

Side 2: The meadows clothe themselves with flocks, the valleys deck themselves with grain; they shout and sing together for joy.
All: We praise you, God, for the harvest of blessings!

GUIDED MEDITATION

Leader: Let us now enter into the memories of our own personal blessings.

Pause after each phrase of the guided meditation.

Close your eyes, breathe deeply and relax. Imagine that you are walking slowly through a grain field. The crop is ready for harvest. A breeze blows gently and the stalks sway. The sun is shining. As you watch, the crop seems to fade away and you are turned back in time to when the field was empty. For as far as you can see there are rows and rows of waiting soil. In the distance there is a lone figure. This person is moving slowly up and down the rows, sowing seed. As the person continues, something remarkable is happening. The seeds are springing up and growing quickly, but they look nothing like grain. Rather, they are the fruits of your labor during this past year. The figure in the distance turns around, and you realize this is you.

Watch yourself observing the field. What has grown the most? What is wilting a little bit? What accomplishment turned out to be your biggest surprise? How can you use what you are about to harvest from the year's work? How much can you share with others? What will the task of harvesting require in energy and resources?

As you watch the field, you are amazed at all that is growing there. A swell of gratitude fills your heart. While the thanksgiving is flowing, something else begins to happen in your field. The sower is not alone anymore. Other figures emerge from between the rows. They are smiling and nodding and moving toward you, carrying baskets. You recognize them as the people who have been significant in your life during this past year: family members, coworkers, neighbors, friends, spiritual companions, acquaintances who made lasting impressions—teachers, guides, children, prophets, challengers, angels. In their baskets they carry the fruits of their encounters with you. You join in their smiling and a warmth fills this place.

It is a sacred place, a holy space, a field of memories, a harvest of good will. These people form a circle, including you, and they set their baskets in the middle. In gratitude for the harvest and for the process that produced it, all of you bow your heads to pray.

Play meditation song: *"There's a Place" by Liam Lawton (GIA).*

Bring the people from the field with you in your heart, and when you feel ready, open your eyes.

Share with those around you some of the most significant blessings of your past year. What has given you joy and enriched your life? What has grown during the past year that you feel ready to harvest now?

Allow time for sharing.

Leader: Having reflected on and shared the blessings of this year for which we are grateful, let us listen to Saint Paul's exhortation to the community of Christians in Philippi.

Reader: Philippians 4:4–9

Leader: With song in our hearts, let us respond to the encouragement Saint Paul gives to the church.

Closing Song: "Deo Gratias" by Peter Rubalcava (OCP)

A Prayer in the Winter Cold
(to value silence and darkness)

Suggestion for atmosphere: a very dark room with a single candle burning.

Opening Song: "God, Beyond All Names" by Bernadette Farrell (OCP)

Leader: In the stillness of this winter night (day), it is good to reflect on how we are bringing God to birth through our living and dying, our daily ups and downs, our joys and sorrows. God has promised to be with us through all our experiences and to be present to us in one another. Jesus prayed, on the night before he died, that all who believe in him would experience unity with one another in a bond of God's love. Let us listen to the words of Jesus in the Gospel of John, and then spend some time in quiet reflection.

Reader: John 17:1–4, 6–8, 13–24

Read slowly; music could be played quietly in the background. Follow the reading with a period of silence. Then the leader begins the psalm.

All: In your light we see light.

PSALM 36:5–10

Side 1: Your steadfast love, O Lord, extends to the heavens, your faithfulness to the clouds.
All: In your light we see light.

Side 2: Your righteousness is like the mighty mountains, your judgments are like the great deep; you save humans and animals alike, O Lord.
All: In your light we see light.

Side 1: How precious is your steadfast love, O God! All people may take refuge in the shadow of your wings.
All: In your light we see light.

Side 2: They feast on the abundance of your house, and you give them drink from the river of your delights.
All: In your light we see light.

Side 1: For with you is the fountain of life; in your light we see light.
All: In your light we see light.

Side 2: O continue your steadfast love to those who know you, and your salvation to the upright of heart!
All: In your light we see light.

Leader: When God's commands were given, through Moses, to the people of Israel, the people received them out of darkness. It was as if they had needed a time away from the light to discover their need for God's guidance. Out of the darkness came directions for how to walk in the light. Let us listen to their experience as Moses describes it.

Reader: Deuteronomy 5:22–24

Leader: Out of the darkness of our winter, we too want guidance for living in the light. Let us pray when the day is dawning on a cold winter morning.
All: Let us walk in the light of the Lord.

Leader: When the last leaves have fallen and cold nips the air.

All: Let us walk in the light of the Lord.

Leader: When stillness descends like a blanket of snow.
All: Let us walk in the light of the Lord.

Leader: Because we are children who trust in our God.
All: We have faith to lead us on.

Leader: Because out of our nighttimes come the fruits of reflection.
All: We have hope to lead us on.

Leader: Because quiet times for renewal can open our hearts.
All: We have love to lead us on.

Leader: When darkness is present and we can't find our way.
All: Let us walk in the light of the Lord.

Leader: When a flickering warmth calls us in from the cold.
All: Let us walk in the light of the Lord.

Leader: When winter challenges us to face life's obstacles.
All: Let us walk in the light of the Lord.

Leader: Because we have seen that seasons change and life grows strong.
All: We have faith to lead us on.

Leader: Because good things happen in darkness and stillness.
All: We have hope to lead us on.

Leader: Because God is the eternal flame at the core of each being.
All: We have love to lead us on.

All: O God of our winter times, we celebrate the vibrancy of your Spirit. In you darkness is not dark, and the cold is only an invitation to fan the flames of renewal. We welcome a season of quiet dormancy, a time to look within for the light that never dims. We bless this season of hibernation and receive it as a gift. Slow our pace that we might value the early arrival of nighttime and its reluctance to give way to morning. For the gifts of winter we praise and thank you. Amen.

Closing Song: "Lord of All Hopefulness" by Timothy R. Smith (OCP)

A Prayer on Presidents' Day
(to request good leaders)

This prayer service could also be used at election time.

Suggestion for atmosphere: *the flag; red, white and blue decor; any national symbols (eagle, etc.).*

Opening Song: "Lord, Every Nation" by Jesse Manibusan (OCP)

Leader: We gather today to pray for our leaders. We are thankful for the good qualities in those who led our country in the past, and we are hopeful that good leaders will step forth to serve in the future. We rely on the Spirit of God who gives gifts for leadership.

Reader: 1 Corinthians 12:4–11

PSALM:72:1–7, 12–15
Side 1: Give the king your justice, O God, and your righteousness to a king's son.
May he judge your people with righteousness, and your poor with justice.
All: We pray for our leaders, O God.

Side 2: May the mountains yield prosperity for the people, and the hills, in righteousness. May he defend the cause of the poor of the people, give deliverance to the needy, and crush the oppressor.
All: We pray for our leaders, O God.

Side 1: May he live while the sun endures, and as long as the moon, throughout all generations.

All: We pray for our leaders, O God.

Side 2: May he be like rain that falls on the mown grass, like showers that water the earth.
All: We pray for our leaders, O God.

Side 1: In his days may righteousness flourish and peace abound, until the moon is no more.
All: We pray for our leaders, O God.

Side 2: For he delivers the needy when they call, the poor and those who have no helper.
All: We pray for our leaders, O God.

Side 1: He has pity on the weak and the needy, and saves the lives of the needy.
All: We pray for our leaders, O God.

Side 2: From oppression and violence he redeems their life; and precious is their blood in his sight.
All: We pray for our leaders, O God.

Side 1: Long may he live! May gold of Sheba be given to him. May prayer be made for him continually; and blessings invoked for him all day long.
All: We pray for our leaders, O God.

Leader: The Gospel tells us about the kind of servant leadership taught and modeled by Jesus. Let us listen and learn.

Reader: Mark 10:35–45

Leader: Jesus said, "Whoever wishes to become great among you must be your servant." Many people have served our country in its history. Some did it better than others, but each had gifts. Whatever each leader did best became a tapestry of talent that gave form and substance to the fabric of our country. Here are just a few descriptions of memorable contributions from our past presidents. As we pray for a continuance of the gifts they manifested, let us remember these leaders with grateful hearts.

Reader: Courage, stamina and leadership during the American Revolution made George Washington a natural choice for the country's first president. He was elected unanimously. The honor embarrassed him, and he preferred to be a farmer at his Mount Vernon estate. But he could not refuse a call to serve. Always dignified, courteous, honest and above scandal, he was a gracious host with a strong personal moral code and a love for animals. He was the first millionaire in the country and, because of his wealth, he did not accept a salary as president.

All: We ask you, Lord, to continue to bless us with leaders who are honest and above reproach. Give us leaders who have a desire to serve without thought for personal gain. We thank you for the courageous and moral leadership our country had when it was beginning. May we nurture kindness, courtesy, moral standards and generosity among our citizens now so that good leaders will emerge for the future.

Reader: Our presidential history has given us blood relatives sometimes. Besides the George Bush family, second and sixth presidents, John Adams and John Quincy Adams, were father and son. Their wife and mother, Abigail Adams, was one of the best-educated women in the country. Through her frequent letters to her husband, she urged attention to women's rights.

William Henry Harrison had the shortest term of office, dying of pneumonia one month after his inauguration, but he was the only president to have a grandson also elected to the office. Benjamin Harrison, serving from 1889 to 1893, installed the first electric lights in the White House.

All: We ask you, Lord, to give us practical and progressive leaders. Give us leaders with open minds and listening hearts and family values. We thank you for past leaders who looked at all sides of the issues, who weren't afraid to make changes, who sought just solutions and equality for citizens. May we nurture close ties in our families and provide support for innovative ideas, so that emerging leaders will be grounded and visionary.

Reader: Thomas Jefferson was interested in everything! From the study of literature, science and law to music, gardening and architectural design, he was an intelligent, gifted, curious person. He experimented with crops, invented versatile furniture and gave elaborate dinner parties. He doubled the size of the country with the Louisiana Purchase and wrote the Declaration of Independence. Jefferson died on the Fourth of July.

All: We ask you, Lord, to continue to bless us with leaders who are intelligent, creative and energetic. Give us leaders who have a variety of interests and abilities and a deep love for freedom and the individual's rights. We thank you for those who crafted the ideals of our democracy. May we nurture goodness in our young, acceptance toward our immigrants and loyalty to causes that are just.

Reader: Our smallest president, James Madison, was a very well-informed person. He delayed making decisions, could be very stubborn, married the legendary hostess Dolley Madison, and is known as the "Father of the Constitution." James Monroe, the first president to tour the country, warned Europe against expanding in America. His warning became the Monroe Doctrine. Jimmy Carter, who never wanted the presidency to be royalty, brought his homespun southern charm and family closeness to the White House. As ex-president, he has remained active in human rights causes and in peacemaking, teaching Sunday school and writing poetry, memoirs, books for young people and historical fiction.

All: We ask you, Lord, to continue to bless us with leaders who are gifted with words, written or spoken, who wisely choose good partners for their life's work, and who honor commitments. Give us leaders who come down from

their "thrones" and walk among us. We thank you for those who captured, in writing, the thoughts in the hearts of many. May we nurture respect for the written words and the selfless acts that have influenced our history and inspired our future leaders.

Reader: Our tallest president, Abraham Lincoln, stands tall in esteem too. This great man was compassionate, tolerant and a good listener. He had a passion for learning and a great skill for storytelling. As president during the Civil War, he issued the proclamation to abolish slavery. There were many who hated him for this, and five days after the war ended, he became the first president to be assassinated. He was fifty-six years old.

Other presidents assassinated in office include James Garfield, age forty-nine; William McKinley, age fifty-eight; John F. Kennedy, age forty-six. Assassination attempts were made against Andrew Jackson and Ronald Reagan.

All: We ask you, Lord, to bless us with leaders who have the courage of their convictions.

Give us leaders who know what they must do, and give them the protection to accomplish their goals safely. We thank you for lives spent working on behalf of others. May we nurture understanding, good mental health and peaceful resolutions of conflict so that citizens of our country will find healthy, safe ways to disagree. We pause now to bless all those who died or were killed while serving in the public forum.

Reader: Theodore Roosevelt greatly increased our national parks, and we continue to value the beauty of our environment and the riches of our resources. Woodrow Wilson and Franklin D. Roosevelt carried the burdens of leadership during the two World Wars, and we continue to find ourselves embroiled in world conflicts for which we need wise, strong and principled leaders. Bill Clinton, known for his empathy and peacemaking skills, desperately wanted to make a difference with his presidency. We still yearn for leaders who set their sights on more than political ambition.

All: We ask you, Lord, to bless us with leaders who have high ideals and the health and stamina to pursue them. Give us leaders who protect our natural resources, who secure our defense and who make an effort to understand how other nations perceive us. We thank you for the way our past leaders helped our nation to cope and to survive when hardship was overwhelming. May we nurture efforts toward peacemaking and tolerance so that not only our country, but also the whole world, may have a future. Amen.

Closing Song: "America the Beautiful" by Katherine L. Bates and Samuel A. Ward

A Prayer When Spring Is Blooming
(to notice and rejoice in life)

Suggestion for atmosphere: Provide seeds and watering cans for a planting ritual to take place as part of the prayer. The prayer can begin indoors and move outside for the planting, or the whole service can take place outside.

Opening Song: "Morning Has Broken" by Eleanor Farjeon (GIA)

MEDITATION

Leader: There is a fresh excitement about the return of spring every year. Whether the winter climate was mild or bitterly cold, there was, in that season, a dormancy that is ending now. We see miracles of life all around us as bulbs push their gifts from the earth, buds puff out greenery on branches, birds build nests with great determination and bushes flower almost overnight.

All this is exciting because it affirms something we know deep inside but which we always seem to want to verify: that life *is* eternal; that what appears to be dead, *isn't;* that renewal is real and ongoing.

What we see all around us resonates in our being: *We* have emerging gifts to share; *we* are bursting with colorful ideas; *we* have great determination to make things happen; and *we* grow in surprising, unexpected ways. Springtime lives in us and is coaxed out of us by the mirrors of life reflecting back to us from our beautiful world.

How will we encourage and protect growth this spring in our fragile selves and in our fragile environment? What can we plant in this season of warmth that will produce fruit in our lives and in our gardens? When can we pause a little in each day to observe the beauty in our inner stirrings and right outside our windows? Where will we hear the sounds of spring if we allow our spirits to sing and the wind to whistle around us?

This is a time for rejoicing and for giving in to hope. This is a time for feeling fully alive. Give yourselves permission to catch spring fever. Become lazy enough to watch the flowers grow.

Pause for reflection.

Reader: Matthew 13:1–9

Response: Psalm 92:1–5, 10, 12–15

Side 1: It is good to give thanks to the Lord, to sing praises to your name, O Most High; to declare your steadfast love in the morning, and your faithfulness by night, to the music of the lute and the harp, to the melody of the lyre.

Side 2: For you, O Lord, have made me glad by your work; at the works of your hands I sing for joy. How great are your works, O Lord! Your thoughts are very deep!

Side 1: But you have exalted my horn like that of the wild ox; you have poured over me fresh oil.

Side 2: The righteous flourish like the palm tree, and grow like a cedar in Lebanon.

Side 1: They are planted in the house of the Lord; they flourish in the courts of our God.

Side 2: In old age they still produce fruit; they are always green and full of sap, showing that the Lord is upright; he is my rock, and there is no unrighteousness in him.

Song: "Lift Up Your Hearts" (verses 1 and 2) by Roc O'Connor, S.J. (OCP)

Leader: We have reflected on the excitement of spring and asked ourselves some challenging questions about our own growth. We listened to Jesus' warning that seeds don't always fall where we want them to be planted, and therefore they might not produce what we are hoping for. The psalm celebrates good people as the seeds that do flourish and bear fruit, and praise is sung to God who plants firmly with love and faithfulness.

We break upon a new day in this new season. Life is calling out to us to participate. Our response to this call will be to plant some seeds and, later, to watch them grow their testimony to life.

Lead the group outside to the planting area if the prayer service began indoors. Involve as many people as possible in the actual planting. After the planting, use questions from the meditation for group sharing:

How will we encourage and protect growth this spring in our fragile selves and in our fragile environment?

What can we plant in this season of warmth that will produce fruit in our lives and in our gardens?

When can we pause a little in each day to observe the beauty in our inner stirrings and right outside our windows?

Where will we hear the sounds of spring if we allow our spirits to sing and the wind to whistle around us?

Reader: John 15:1–5

Response: Isaiah 5:1–2, 7

Side 1: Let me sing for my beloved my love song concerning his vineyard:

Side 2: My beloved had a vineyard on a very fertile hill. He dug it and cleared it of stones, and planted it with choice vines;

Side 1: He built a watchtower in the midst of it and hewed out a wine vat in it; he expected it to yield grapes;

Side 2: For the vineyard of the Lord of hosts is the house of Israel, and the people of Judah are his pleasant planting.

All: As we grow on the vine of your family, Lord, keep us grafted to you and make us productive. Put the song of spring in our hearts, and let us believe that each new day holds promise for our development. May the seeds we planted today be reminders of our call to grow. Amen.

Closing Song: "Lift Up Your Hearts" (all verses), by Roc O'Connor, S.J. (OCP)

A Prayer on July Fourth
(to celebrate freedom)

Suggestion for atmosphere: symbols of liberty: picture of Liberty Bell, news articles/pictures about released captives, open handcuffs, signs saying "Freedom," poster collage of pictures and phrases expressing liberty, etc.

Opening Song: "In the Day of the Lord" (verses 1, 2 and 3) by M.D. Ridge (OCP)

Leader: Freedom is a fierce need, so fierce that battles have been waged to procure it. The focal point of Jewish history in our Old Testament is the Exodus event, the story of the Hebrew people's release from slavery in Egypt.

Reader: Exodus 12:37–42

Response: Psalm 78:1–4, 12–16, 54–55, 69–72

Side 1: Give ear, O my people, to my teaching; incline your ears to the words of my mouth.

Side 2: I will open my mouth in a parable; I will utter dark sayings from of old, things that we have heard and known, that our ancestors have told us.

Side 1: We will not hide them from their children; we will tell to the coming generation the glorious deeds of the Lord, and his might and the wonders that he has done.

Side 2: In the sight of their ancestors he worked marvels in the land of Egypt, in the fields of Zoan.

Side 1: He divided the sea and let them pass through it, and made the waters stand like a heap.

Side 2: In the daytime he led them with a cloud, and all night long with a fiery light.

Side 1: He split rocks open in the wilderness, and gave them drink abundantly as from the deep.

Side 2: He made streams come out of the rock, and caused waters to flow down like rivers.

Side 1: And he brought them to his holy hill, to the mountain that his right hand had won.

Side 2: He drove out nations before them; he apportioned them for a possession and settled the tribes of Israel in their tents.

Side 1: He built his sanctuary like the high heavens, like the earth, which he has founded forever.

Side 2: He chose his servant David, and took him from the sheepfolds; from tending the nursing ewes he brought him to be the shepherd of his people Jacob, of Israel, his inheritance.

Side 1: With upright heart he tended them, and guided them with skillful hand.

Reader: Virginia Smith, author of *God for Grownups*, writes about the use and abuse of freedom. She says:

> Human beings are created to think, speak, act, and live as free people. Americans should have no trouble absorbing this; the nation was founded on precisely this precept. But, as with free will, there are all manner of ways in which human freedom can be abused, and, as history attests, nearly all of them have been exercised at one time or another.
>
> Freedom, then, is not license, a total disregard for restraint. When that which I am entitled to collides with that which you are entitled to, something's got to give. There arises a need for a mutually agreeable restriction of a legal or moral nature.[2]

Pause to reflect on the differences between freedom and license.

Leader: Many people are seeking freedom today: teenagers moving toward independence, women seeking to abolish the restrictions that have left them less free than men, minority groups wanting to exercise the same rights given to majority groups, nations threatened by other nations, people oppressed by their own governments. Some know what freedom is, but don't know how to obtain it. Some equate freedom with "anything goes." Some confuse granting freedom with wielding power. Some have suffered the loss of freedom for so long that they don't have any hope of experiencing it.

Let us pray for the people and groups who are not free. As these people are named, we will all respond, "Lord, lead them to freedom."

Allow time for spontaneous naming from the group.

Let us pray for the people and groups who are helping others to secure freedom. As these people are named, we will all respond, "Lord, be with them and bless their efforts."

Allow time for spontaneous naming from the group.

All: Freedom is a precious right and we ask you to keep us free, Lord. Even as we ask, may we be aware that freedom's restrictions and responsibilities arise out of respect for the freedom of others. Help us to be consciously aware of our self-centered strivings. Open our eyes to see where others are struggling for their freedom. Make us generous in assisting the people who work daily for the rights of all human beings. Amen.

Leader: Let us celebrate freedom, remembering those who fought to keep us free. Let us celebrate freedom, thanking those who taught us to be gracious about our rights. Let us celebrate freedom, seeking ways to bring freedom to those who don't have it. Let us celebrate freedom in loud, joyful ways and in quiet, reflective ways. Let freedom ring!

Closing Song: "In the Day of the Lord" (verses 4, 5 and 6), M.D. Ridge (OCP)

A Prayer in the Summer Warmth
(to rejoice in leisure and renewal)

Suggestion for atmosphere: *a fan to blow lightly on participants during the guided imagery experience; a tape of bird sounds, breezes, water, summer storm, etc.*

Opening Song: "Come to Me" by Gregory Norbert, O.S.B. (Weston Priory, Benedictine Foundation)

Leader: You are invited to come into a restful place. Jesus encouraged his disciples to take time away from their work, to rest and renew themselves. Jesus, too, went apart from people sometimes to pray and to prepare himself for upcoming tasks and decisions.

Reader: Mark 6:30–32

Leader: It is interesting that we find Jesus' exhortation to rest in the Gospel of Mark. This is the Gospel that presents Jesus as a man of action, always on the move toward Jerusalem, having a sense of urgency about accomplishing his goal there. Jesus is surrounded by crowds and feeling a lot of pressure, sometimes discouraged by his disciples' slowness to understand who he is and what he is about. Yet in the midst of all the work, he does tell his followers to come away and rest.

Our lives are busy too, and we don't often give ourselves permission to relax. But summer is the season that beckons us to change the pace, back off a little from the work, tone down the intensity. So let's do that now for a little while. Just come away and rest.

GUIDED MEDITATION

Play a tape of nature sounds quietly in the background; turn on a fan.

Leader: Close your eyes, breathe deeply and relax. You are in your favorite outdoor summer vacation spot. Relax completely in this place. Feel your muscles loosen and the tension drop away. The sun is warm on your face and a light breeze gently touches your skin. Listen to the natural sounds of creatures and elements. Experience the peace of being totally immersed in your special place. As you relax, become aware that Jesus has joined you. He is silent, waiting for whatever you would like to say. Enjoy the silence, then speak what is in your heart.

Pause.

Jesus understands and responds. Your conversation continues back and forth until you both fall silent again.

Pause.

Once more you become aware of the natural sounds around you. Jesus comments on the beauty of the surroundings and commends you for recognizing God's gift to you in this place. He tells you that summertime is part of God's plan: for people and creatures to rest, renew, relate, recover, play, plan, dream and heal. Jesus gives you a blessing and encourages you to come often to this favorite summer place.

You are alone again and notice, one more time, the sounds and the sun, the breeze and the peace.

When you are ready, open your eyes.

Leader: While holding the memory of this experience, let us pray Psalm 84.

Side 1: How lovely is your dwelling place, O Lord of hosts! My soul longs, indeed it faints for the courts of the Lord; my heart and my flesh sing for joy to the living God.

Side 2: Even the sparrow finds a home, and the swallow a nest for herself, where she may lay her young, at your altars, O Lord of hosts, my King and my God.

Side 1: Happy are those who live in your house, ever singing your praise. Happy are those whose strength is in you, in whose heart are the highways to Zion.

Side 2: As they go through the valley of Baca they make it a place of springs; the early rain also covers it with pools. They go from strength to strength; the God of gods will be seen in Zion.

Side 1: O Lord God of hosts, hear my prayer; give ear, O God of Jacob! Behold our shield, O God; look on the face of your anointed.

Side 2: For a day in your courts is better than a thousand elsewhere. I would rather be a door-keeper in the house of my God than live in the tents of wickedness.

Side 1: For the Lord God is a sun and shield; he bestows favor and honor.

Side 2: No good thing does the Lord withhold from those who walk uprightly. O Lord of hosts, happy is everyone who trusts in you.

All: Jesus, as we return often to dwell in our summer place, be with us there. Teach us how to hear your voice when we allow you time to speak. Renew our spirits when we seek refreshment in your presence. Help us believe that quiet moments are productive, not wasted. Let us be willing to "waste" time with you. Amen.

Closing Song: "Fly Like a Bird" by Ken Canedo (Lorenz)

PART III

✛

Praying With Special Saints

Praying With Saint Valentine on February 14

Suggestion for atmosphere: Valentine cards, red hearts, Valentine's Day fabric for a table cover, red and white candles, empty basket; materials for use during the prayer: red construction paper, white note paper, scissors, tape, colored marking pens.

Opening Song: "Rain Down" by Jaime Cortez (OCP)

Leader: How good it is to have a special day just for expressing love! This day takes its name from the saint who, as bishop, loved and cared for his people and, as martyr, remained faithful to loving God even when persecuted. Our custom of giving "valentines" comes from the story of Saint Valentine sending notes, while in prison, to those he cared for. He wanted to encourage them to keep faith.

Love comes from God. Our ability to reach out to others is a gift. We are able to celebrate our ability to love. We begin by listening to Saint Paul define it:

Reader: 1 Corinthians 13:1–13

Response: Psalm 112:1–9

Leader: Praise the Lord! Happy are those who fear the Lord, who greatly delight in his commandments. Their descendants will be mighty in the land; the generation of the upright will be blessed.
All: Our hearts are firm, secure in the Lord.

Leader: Wealth and riches are in their houses, and their righteousness endures forever. They rise in the darkness as a light for the upright; they are gracious, merciful and righteous.
All: Our hearts are firm, secure in the Lord.

Leader: It is well with those who deal generously and lend, who conduct their affairs with justice. For the righteous will never be moved; they will be remembered forever.
All: Our hearts are firm, secure in the Lord.

Leader: They are not afraid of evil tidings; their hearts are firm, secure in the Lord. Their hearts are steady, they will not be afraid; in the end they will look in triumph on their foes.
All: Our hearts are firm, secure in the Lord.

Leader: They have distributed freely, they have given to the poor; their righteousness endures forever; their horn is exalted in honor.
All: Our hearts are firm, secure in the Lord.

Leader: Saint John, too, says that love is measured by our actions.

Reader: 1 John 3:14–23

Leader: Saint Paul and Saint John have challenged us by their exhortations to actively love others. You will have some quiet time now to do two things.

Write a note to God expressing your love and gratitude. Include some specific ways you will honor God by showing love to others. Later, everyone will place the notes in the basket as an offering.

Create a valentine for someone to whom you want to express your love. This could include a promise of something you want to do for this person. You will take this with you to deliver it after you leave here.

Provide materials and allow time for the writing and card making. When all are finished, the leader begins the litany:

Leader: Bishop Valentine, you took responsibility for a flock of believers, and love kept you mindful of their needs. You gave an example of how to lead by loving.
All: Saint Valentine, help us grow in love.

Leader: You looked upon your role in the church as an opportunity to serve.
All: Saint Valentine, help us grow in love.

Leader: You gave an example of how to make God the central focus of our lives.
All: Saint Valentine, help us grow in love.

Leader: Compassionate Valentine, you were aware of the needs of people in your community and you reached out to them. That we may remember to show others how much we care.
All: Saint Valentine, inspire us.

Leader: That we may remember to be generous to those in need.
All: Saint Valentine, inspire us.

Leader: That we may remember to show our love through service.
All: Saint Valentine, inspire us.

Leader: Prisoner Valentine, you wrote messages of encouragement to your Christian community—love letters from your jail cell. As we make efforts to encourage those we love,
All: Saint Valentine, be with us.

Leader: As we give and receive cards pledging our love,
All: Saint Valentine, be with us.

Leader: As we sometimes give up our personal freedom while choosing to love,
All: Saint Valentine, be with us.

Leader: Martyr Valentine, you chose to die rather than to compromise your beliefs, holding on to faith and loving God above all. When we face challenges to our love,
All: Saint Valentine, pray for us.

Leader: When fear tempts us to betray our values,
All: Saint Valentine, pray for us.

Leader: When we are called to risk all in the name of love,
All: Saint Valentine, pray for us.

Leader: As we sing our closing song, bring your love letter to God and place it in the basket. After the song ends, go in love and peace to deliver your Valentine message and to follow your hearts.

Closing Song: "We Gotta Love" by Tom Booth, Israel Houghton, Matt Maher (OCP)

Praying With Saint Patrick on March 17

Suggestion for atmosphere: shamrocks and/or Saint Patrick's Day fabric for the table, green and white candles, shamrock plant, picture or statue of Saint Patrick, Celtic cross.

Opening Song: "Irish Blessing" (verses 1, 2 and 3) by Bob Fabing, s.j. (OCP)

Leader: We honor Saint Patrick today as the beloved saint who brought Christianity to Ireland. Although he was kidnapped as a young boy and brought against his will to Ireland, he learned to love the Celtic people. Later, after returning home, he freely chose to return to the Emerald Isle as a missionary. As a bishop, he ordained priests and founded monasteries. Christianity blossomed throughout the island because of his passionate dedication.

This passage from the Gospel of Luke might have been a source of inspiration for Patrick. Certainly it calls us to his kind of commitment.

Reader: Luke 18:18–30

Response: Isaiah 63:7–9, 14

Reader: I will recount the gracious deeds of the Lord, the praiseworthy acts of the Lord, because of all that the Lord has done for us, and the great favor to the house of Israel that he has shown them according to his mercy, according to the abundance of his steadfast love.
All: To the nations you send your message, Lord.

Reader: For he said, "Surely they are my people, children who will not deal falsely"; and he became their savior in all their distress.
All: To the nations you send your message, Lord.

Reader: It was no messenger or angel but his presence that saved them; in his love and in his pity he redeemed them; he lifted them up and carried them all the days of old.
All: To the nations you send your message, Lord.

Reader: Like cattle that go down into the valley, the spirit of the Lord gave them rest. Thus you led your people, to make for yourself a glorious name.
All: To the nations you send your message, Lord.

Leader: Patrick believed that the message of Christ needed to reach the people of Ireland, much like Saint Paul believed that the Gospel was for Gentiles as well as Jews.

Reader: Romans 15:7–13

Leader: Dear Patrick, missionary to the people of Ireland, we celebrate today your triumph over life's setbacks. When taken from your people, you made a new people your own. After experiencing slavery, you freely chose to return to those you had learned to love. Through the examples you give us of courage, forgiveness, faith and love, we hope to find our way to live into God's plan for us. We call on you for assistance.
All: Saint Patrick, intercede for us.

Leader: When life takes us in directions we did not choose,
All: Saint Patrick, intercede for us.

Leader: When doubts and fears attempt to be our companions,
All: Saint Patrick, intercede for us.

Leader: When we seek a way to share what we believe,
All: Saint Patrick, intercede for us.

Leader: As travelers on a road with many turns, we pray,
All: Saint Patrick, intercede for us.

Leader: As seekers of wisdom pursuing ever-clearer insights, we pray,
All: Saint Patrick, intercede for us.

Leader: As people who want to follow Christ faithfully, we pray,
All: Saint Patrick, intercede for us.

Leader: For the grace to be light-hearted when burdens are heavy,
All: Saint Patrick, intercede for us.

Leader: For the gift of telling stories to preserve our past,
All: Saint Patrick, intercede for us.

Leader: For the spirit of prayer to discern God's will for our journey,
All: Saint Patrick, intercede for us.

Leader: In the quiet moments that follow, let us touch the faith of our ancestors rooted and blooming in our own hearts. Let us be grateful for this gift.

Play music during the quiet period. One suggestion: "Breastplate" by Liam Lawton (GIA) from the album In the Quiet.

Leader: Saint Patrick relied on Christ, honored the Trinity and cherished God's creation. In his memory, let us pray.

All: O God, who is Three-in-One, we call on you to make us strong in faith, cheerful in hope, radiant in love. We see you in the world you made: bright sun, mighty wind, deep sea, firm earth, steep rock, radiant moon. Stand between us and the powers of darkness so your protection will shield us from all harm. We pray this in the name of Christ. Amen.

Closing Song: "Irish Blessing" (verses 4, 5 and 6) by Bob Fabing, s.j. (OCP)

Praying With Saint Catherine of Siena on April 29

Suggestion for atmosphere: picture of Saint Catherine, candle, small signs lettered with these words: Mystic, Diplomat, Negotiator, Dominican, Preacher, Spiritual Director, Reformer, Prison Minister, Servant.

Opening Song: "Taste and See" by James E. Moore, Jr. (GIA)

Leader: As we celebrate the holiness of Saint Catherine, we want to be aware that she, like Saint Paul, suffered persecution for her efforts on behalf of the church. Mystic that she was, she found strength through her union with Jesus.

Reader: 2 Corinthians 11:30–31; 12:1–10

Response: Psalm 34:1–9, 11–18, 22

Side 1: I will bless the Lord at all times; his praise shall continually be in my mouth. My soul makes its boast in the Lord; let the humble hear and be glad.
Side 2: O magnify the Lord with me, and let us exalt his name together. I sought the Lord, and he answered me, and delivered me from all my fears.

Side 1: Look to him, and be radiant; so your faces shall never be ashamed. This poor soul cried, and was heard by the Lord, and was saved from every trouble.
Side 2: The angel of the Lord encamps around those who fear him, and delivers them. O taste and see that the Lord is good; happy are those who take refuge in him.

Side 1: O fear the Lord, you his holy ones, for those who fear him have no want. Come, O children, listen to me; I will teach you the fear of the Lord.

Side 2: Which of you desires life, and covets many days to enjoy good? Keep your tongue from evil, and your lips from speaking deceit. Depart from evil, and do good; seek peace and pursue it.

Side 1: The eyes of the Lord are on the righteous, and his ears are open to their cry. The face of the Lord is against evildoers, to cut off the remembrance of them from the earth.
Side 2: When the righteous cry for help, the Lord hears, and rescues them from all their troubles. The Lord is near to the brokenhearted, and saves the crushed in spirit. The Lord redeems the life of his servants; none of those who take refuge in him will be condemned.

Leader: As a prelude to the meditation we will enter into tonight, let us listen to the Beatitudes which surely must have moved Catherine to her work of peacemaking, tending to the poor and negotiating reforms in church leadership.

Reader: Matthew 5:3–12

Response: Psalm 63:1–8

Side 1: O God, you are my God, I seek you, my soul thirsts for you; my flesh faints for you, as in a dry and weary land where there is no water. So I have looked upon you in the sanctuary, beholding your power and glory.
Side 2: Because your steadfast love is better than life, my lips will praise you. So I will bless you as long as I live; I will lift up my hands and call on your name.

Side 1: My soul is satisfied as with a rich feast, and my mouth praises you with joyful lips when I think of you on my bed, and meditate on you in the watches of the night.
Side 2: For you have been my help, and in the shadow of your wings I sing for joy. My soul clings to you; your right hand upholds me.

Leader: We celebrate saints because of what they teach us about loving God and about using our life to make a difference. Saint Catherine of Siena, though only thirty-three when she died, accomplished such significant things with her life that people refer to her now as a mystic, a peacemaker, a servant of the poor and a spokesperson for church reform.

Picture the fourteenth-century Italian custom of men choosing husbands for the women in their families and a young girl who resisted her brothers' pressure to marry any suitor they brought in. From a very young age, Catherine pledged her life to Jesus and experienced visions through which Jesus gave her guidance and direction.

Picture this member of the Dominican laity, reluctantly leaving her beloved solitude and her experiences of mystical union with Christ to go out as God directed her. She was sent to find Christ among the poor and suffering, to tend to their needs in hospitals and even to accompany and comfort prisoners as they prepared for execution. Picture Catherine eventually founding a monastery of Dominican Sisters.

Picture a Christian church in the Western world, not yet divided by the Protestant Reformation, but very divided on the question of leadership. A French pope ruled from Avignon, France, to avoid arguments with Italians. Catherine persuaded him to return to Rome. She lived through the Western Schism that followed, when opposing factions put forth rival popes. An assassin tried to kill her during the violence of those troubled times.

Picture an uneducated woman with twenty-three older siblings, who grew up to become the spiritual director of scholarly men. She dictated letters to church leaders to encourage reform. She dictated a book about her mystical experiences to witness to God's love. She negotiated, with moral authority, to bring peace to her troubled church.

We are inspired by Catherine's life because she grounded herself in prayer and then acted on her convictions. Let us pause now to reflect on the ways we have opened ourselves to God's grace while we live in an age that has its own turmoil:

What choices have you made with your life? Did anyone influence those choices or try to prevent them?

What kind of prayer life have you developed? How has your prayer moved you to take some action?

What are the conflicts, disagreements and problems in the church today? What are you doing about them to encourage needed reforms?

Let us pray:

All: We thank you, God, for people like Saint Catherine, who show us that with you, we can do anything and without you, we can do nothing. Call us to union with you. Call us to make time for you. Fill us with your love so completely that it will overflow from us to those we touch. Make us mystics in the service of Jesus. Amen.

Closing Song: "My God and My All" by Rufino Zaragoza, O.F.M. (OCP)

Praying With Saint Francis of Assisi on October 4

Suggestion for atmosphere: *San Damiano cross, statue of Saint Francis, fall flowers, candle, forest creatures, nature scenes, fountain, signs from the Canticle to mark some of the items (Brother Sun, Sister Moon, Brother Wind, Sister Water, Brother Fire, Sister Earth).*

Put the cross and the statue on a table in the front of the prayer space. Place the signs, standing up, at various places on the table. During the opening song, designate six people to walk in carrying objects to place by the signs: picture of the sun, picture of moon and stars, picture of trees bending in wind or a windmill, bowl of water or a tabletop water fountain, a lighted candle, potted flowers.

Opening Song: "Canticle of the Sun" by Marty Haugen (GIA)

Leader: Saint Francis is known for his love of all creation. People, animals, plants, the sun, water, birds, everything! Whether he was taming a wolf, embracing a leper or making peace between a bishop and a mayor, Francis sincerely loved everyone and clearly saw God in everything. His well-known Canticle, in which he sang of everything as brother and sister, was actually composed near the end of his life while his eyes were experiencing intense agony from the sun. That pain did not dampen the joy of his remembering God's beautiful world.

In the spirit of Saint Francis' love for the earth, let us pray Psalm 104:

PSALM 104:1–24, 31–34, 35B

Side 1: Bless the Lord, O my soul; O Lord my God, you are very great. You are clothed with honor and majesty, wrapped in light as with a garment.

Side 2: You stretch out the heavens like a tent, you set the beams of your chambers on the waters, you make the clouds your chariot, you ride on the wings of the wind.

Side 1: You make the winds your messengers, fire and flame your ministers. You set the earth on its foundations, so that it shall never be shaken.

Side 2: You cover it with the deep as with a garment; the waters stood above the mountains. At your rebuke they flee; at the sound of your thunder they take to flight.

Side 1: They rose up to the mountains, ran down to the valleys to the place that you appointed for them. You set a boundary that they may not pass, so that they might not again cover the earth.

Side 2: You make springs gush forth in the valleys; they flow between the hills, giving drink to every wild animal; the wild asses quench their thirst.

Side 1: By the streams the birds of the air have their habitation; they sing among the branches. From your lofty abode you water the mountains; the earth is satisfied with the fruit of your work.

Side 2: You cause the grass to grow for the cattle, and plants for people to use, to bring forth food from the earth, and wine to gladden the human heart, oil to make the face shine, and bread to strengthen the human heart.

Side 1: The trees of the Lord are watered abundantly, the cedars of Lebanon that he planted. In them the birds build their nests; the stork has its home in the fir trees.

Side 2: The high mountains are for the wild goats; the rocks are a refuge for the coneys. You have made the moon to mark the seasons; the sun knows its time for setting.

Side 1: You make darkness, and it is night, when all the animals of the forest come creeping out. The young lions roar for their prey, seeking their food from God.

Side 2: When the sun rises, they withdraw and lie down in their dens. People go out to their work and to their labor until the evening.

Side 1: O Lord, how manifold are your works! In wisdom you have made them all; the earth is full of your creatures.

Side 2: May the glory of the Lord endure forever; may the Lord rejoice in his works—who looks on the earth and it trembles, who touches the mountains and they smoke.

Side 1: I will sing to the Lord as long as I live; I will sing praise to my God while I have being.

Side 2: May my meditation be pleasing to him, for I rejoice in the Lord. Bless the Lord, O my soul.

Leader: In the early days of Francis' religious fervor, when his brothers in the spirit sought to join him, he chose the rules for their lives in community by randomly opening the Scriptures three times. This is what he read:

Reader: Matthew 19:21; 16:24–25; Mark 6:8–9

Have the passages marked ahead of time and then open the Bible three separate times to read them.

All: Jesus, your servant Saint Francis was a humble, simple man who understood your message. He gave up a life of luxury and committed himself to living among and serving the poor. Because he wholeheartedly embraced the gospel, you filled him with immeasurable joy. Touch us with the fervor of Francis. Help us to be as willing to follow you as he was.

Leader: Franciscan friar Murray Bodo, in his book *Tales of Saint Francis,* concludes his many stories about Francis with these words:

Reader:

It is not what Francis did in the Church, then, that is so important, but the image that Francis and his followers became. They imaged what the Church and each individual Christian can be. He held up an icon that people recognized as a mirror both of Christ and of themselves, provided they were indeed what they were meant to be. And the more Francis lived the Gospel literally and radically, the clearer the picture became. And that is the secret of the tales of Francis of Assisi. They show us a living, moving, breathing image of Jesus Christ, and that alone draws people to God. No amount of teaching and preaching, of directives and censures, of encyclical letters of reform like those of the Popes of his time or ours, can substitute for a human being become Christ to his or her age.[3]

All: Saint Francis, you looked upon the cross of Jesus and allowed the image to speak to your heart. You took up your own cross, often ridiculed for enthusiastically proclaiming a life of self-denial. You allowed God to work through you to speak messages of peace and reconciliation to a troubled church and a divided world. As we remember you today, bless us with your passion for following Jesus.

Leader: In the spirit of all that called to Francis and moved him with compassion, let us present our petitions to God.

In memory of Francis' visit to the pope, we pray for our church, that her leaders may be open to the messages God sends them through simple signs and holy people, we pray to the Lord.

All: Lord, hear our prayer.

Leader: In memory of Francis' encounter with a leper, we pray for society's outcasts, that they may find in us someone to understand and help them, we pray to the Lord.

All: Lord, hear our prayer.

Leader: In memory of Francis' visit to the Sultan, we pray for Christians and Muslims that we may be willing to dialogue and to respect each other's beliefs, we pray to the Lord.

All: Lord, hear our prayer.

Leader: In memory of Francis taming a wolf, we pray for people who are governed by their fears, that they may turn away from violent solutions and move toward peaceful understanding, we pray to the Lord.

All: Lord, hear our prayer.

Leader: In memory of Francis embracing poverty, we pray for our consumer society, that we may convert our materialistic values to a greater awareness of the world's need increased by our greed, we pray to the Lord.

All: Lord, hear our prayer.

Leader: In memory of Francis' love for all creation, we pray for those who care for the environment, that they may persevere in their efforts to preserve species and resources and to educate the unaware, we pray to the Lord.

All: Lord, hear our prayer.

Leader: Let us pray:

All: God, hear the prayers we offer today as we reflect on the needs of our world, so like the world of Francis which also needed peace and compassion. May this feast we celebrate bring us to a conversion of heart so that we, too, will become peacemakers and lovers of the gospel of Jesus. Help us to simplify our lives and open our eyes. Amen.

Closing Song: "Prayer of Saint Francis" by Sebastian Temple (OCP)

Praying With All Saints on November 1

Suggestion for atmosphere: Make this an experience for children in the parish, to encourage them to celebrate Halloween as "Hallowed Eve." Plan an evening prayer service on October 31, working ahead of time with the children to decorate pumpkins as favorite saints. (Study saints and their symbols.) Bring the finished pumpkins to the prayer space and light candles around them (or in them). Children can also be encouraged to wear saint costumes. Have a party after the prayer.

Opening Song: "I Am the Light of the World" by Greg Hayakawa (OCP)

Children process in wearing costumes. Music plays as background until they are in their places. Then invite everyone to sing.

Leader: This is a very special night. We are honoring all the saints because they show us how to follow Jesus. Jesus told his followers not to worry about anything because God loves them and will take care of them. Saints believed this. And Jesus told people to give up things and share with others. That's what helps the kingdom of God to come on earth. Saints did this too. Let's listen to the Gospel story where Jesus teaches these things.

Reader: Luke 12:22–34

Leader: Now we will pray Psalm 89. After each part, respond: "We love you, God."

PSALM 89:1–9, 11–17

Leader: I will sing of your steadfast love, O Lord, forever; with my mouth I will proclaim your faithfulness to all generations. I declare that your steadfast love is established forever; your faithfulness is as firm as the heavens.
All: We love you, God.

Leader: You said, "I have made a covenant with my chosen one, I have sworn to my servant David: 'I will establish your descendants forever, and build your throne for all generations.'"
All: We love you, God.

Leader: Let the heavens praise your wonders, O Lord, your faithfulness in the assembly of the holy ones.
All: We love you, God.

Leader: For who in the skies can be compared to the Lord? Who among the heavenly beings is like the Lord, a God feared in the council of the holy ones, great and awesome above all that are around him?
All: We love you, God.

Leader: Lord God of hosts, who is as mighty as you, O Lord? Your faithfulness surrounds you. You rule the raging of the sea; when its waves rise, you still them.
All: We love you, God.

Leader: The heavens are yours, the earth also is yours; the world and all that is in it—you have founded them.
All: We love you, God.

Leader: The north and the south—you created them; Tabor and Hermon joyously praise your name. You have a mighty arm; strong is your hand, high your right hand.
All: We love you, God.

Leader: Righteousness and justice are the foundation of your throne; steadfast love and faithfulness go before you. Happy are the people who know the festal shout, who walk, O Lord, in the light of your countenance.
All: We love you, God.

Leader: They exult in your name all day long, and extol your righteousness. For you are the glory of their strength; by your favor our horn is exalted.
All: We love you, God.

Leader: On this special feast day, the saints are probably having a big party in heaven. Mostly they are celebrating how much God loves them. The person who wrote the Book of Revelation in the Bible tried to imagine what that scene in heaven would look like. Here is what that person wrote:

Reader: Revelation 7:9–17

After the reading, invite children to come forward to explain the pumpkins they decorated. Who is the saint? What did that saint do? What does that saint teach us? When the children are finished, the leader continues:

Leader: Let us call on the saints now to help us do good things like they did. When I point to you, say "Pray for us." Saints of the Old Testament, prophets and leaders who encouraged people to be faithful to God:

Reader: Liberators Moses and Miriam, judges Samuel and Deborah, King Hezekiah and Queen Esther, prophets Isaiah and Jeremiah, and all holy people in the history of our salvation,
All: Pray for us.

Leader: Saints of the New Testament, leaders in the early days of the Church, who helped people remember the teachings of Jesus:

Reader: Peter and James, apostles; Mary Magdalene and Joanna, disciples; Paul and Barnabas missionaries; Lydia and Priscilla, who housed local churches; Matthew, Mark, Luke, John, evangelists; Mary, the mother of Jesus; and all holy people who spread the Christian message,
All: Pray for us.

Leader: Martyrs throughout history, who gave up their lives rather than their faith and good works:

Reader: Bishops Blase and Valentine, the February saints of throat blessings and love notes; noblewoman Perpetua and slavewoman Felicity, beheaded in the ancient Roman Empire; Thomas More and John Fisher, executed in London Tower; Joan of Arc, burned at the stake in France; Archbishop Romero and the women missionaries murdered in El Salvador; and all holy people whose courage kept them faithful to their beliefs,
All: Pray for us.

Leader: Founders of religious orders, who formed communities of people who would pray, teach, and serve:

Reader: Benedict and Scholastica, twins who founded communities five miles apart; Dominic, founder of the Dominicans; Francis and Clare, founders of Franciscan communities of men and women; Ignatius, founder of the Jesuits; Angela Merici, foundress of the first teaching order and first secular institute; and all holy people who gathered others around them to do good works,
All: Pray for us.

Leader: Patron saints whose lives became a model and an inspiration for certain countries:

Reader: Patrick and Brigid, patron saints of Ireland; Andrew, patron saint of Scotland and Russia; Agnes, patron saint of Malta; Stephen, patron saint of Hungary; Gertrude, patron saint of the West Indies; Francis Xavier, patron saint of Japan; and all holy people who inspired nations to follow the way of Christ,
All: Pray for us.

Leader: Patron saints whose lives became a model and an inspiration for certain professions or groups:

Reader: Monica, patron saint of mothers; Nicholas, patron saint of children; Joseph, patron saint of fathers; Cecilia, patron saint of musicians; Jerome, patron saint of librarians; Louise de Marillac, patron saint of social workers; and all holy people who have become an inspiration to others through their work,
All: Pray for us.

Leader: Contemporary people, not yet canonized whom we honor as saints because of their holy lives:

Reader: Pope John XXIII, opening the window for church renewal; Mother Teresa of Calcutta, serving the poor in India; Thomas Merton, contemplative Trappist monk; Dorothy Day, courageous witness to the gospel; Thea Bowman, African American liturgist; Teilhard de Chardin, scientist of the cosmos; and all holy people today who are following the call of Jesus,

All: Pray for us.

Leader: Let us remember that November 1 is a very special day, and the eve of November 1 is a very special night, because we remember that throughout history many wonderful people have shown us how to live good lives. We end our prayer tonight asking Jesus to be the light in our hearts so we will live like saints too.

Closing Song: "Christ, Be Our Light" by Bernadette Farrell (OCP)

Praying With the Martyrs of El Salvador on December 2

Suggestion for atmosphere: pictures of the missionary women: Jean Donovan, Sister Ita Ford, Sister Maura Clarke, Sister Dorothy Kazel, or pictures of poor people in Central America; a candle.

Opening Song: "The Cry of the Poor" by John Foley, S.J. (OCP)

Leader: On December 2, 1980, Maryknoll missionary Sisters Ita Ford and Maura Clarke, Ursuline Sister Dorothy Kazel and lay missionary Jean Donovan were brutally raped and murdered in El Salvador. They knew their names were on the death lists circulated by a government that was intimidating, torturing and killing its people. But these women did not abandon the poor people they had come to serve. They believed the Lord hears the cry of the poor.

First Reader: Matthew 10:16–23

Response: Psalm 94:2–22

Side 1: Rise up, O judge of the earth; give to the proud what they deserve! O Lord, how long shall the wicked, how long shall the wicked exult?
Side 2: They pour out their arrogant words; all the evildoers boast. They crush your people, O Lord, and afflict your heritage.

Side 1: They kill the widow and the stranger, they murder the orphan, and they say, "The Lord does not see; the God of Jacob does not perceive."
Side 2: Understand, O dullest of the people; fools, when will you be wise? He who planted the ear, does he not hear? He who formed the eye, does he not see?

Side 1: He who disciplines the nations, he who teaches knowledge to humankind, does he not chastise? The Lord knows our thoughts, that they are but an empty breath.
Side 2: Happy are those whom you discipline, O Lord, and whom you teach out of your law, giving them respite from days of trouble, until a pit is dug for the wicked.

Side 1: For the Lord will not forsake his people; he will not abandon his heritage; for justice will return to the righteous, and all the upright in heart will follow it.
Side 2: Who rises up for me against the wicked? Who stands up for me against evildoers? If the Lord had not been my help, my soul would soon have lived in the land of silence.

Side 1: When I thought, "My foot is slipping," your steadfast love, O Lord, held me up. When the cares of my heart are many, your consolations cheer my soul.
Side 2: Can wicked rulers be allied with you, those who contrive mischief by statute? They band together against the life of the righteous, and condemn the innocent to death. But the Lord has become my stronghold, and my God the rock of my refuge.

Leader: A beautiful TV movie, produced in the 1980s, called *Choices of the Heart,* told the story of Jean Donovan as she struggled to find the way God wanted her to serve. Melissa Gilbert depicted Jean's zest for life, her courage and indomitable spirit, her questions about faith, her admiration of Archbishop Romero and her love for the people of El Salvador.

As the story unfolded, the viewer came to know Jean and the Sisters who were her missionary companions even through death. The choices of their hearts led them to give up comfortable, safe lives and to choose to remain with a people struggling for justice, living in fear, dying under false accusations. Their association with these people brought them to martyrdom less than a year after Archbishop Romero was murdered. These women faced their fears, remained loyal to the oppressed who needed their voice, and suffered the pain of those who choose to follow Christ.

Not all of us are called to martyrdom, but we are called to make choices of the heart. Having the example of people who search for meaning, question their faith, decide between options, reach outward in love and place trust in God, inspires us to be noble with our lives too. We look to the martyrs of El Salvador as people who call forth the best in us. Like them we can choose to be generous, loving and selfless. Like them we can choose to be aware of the needs in our world today.

All: Lord, give us the courage to stand with the oppressed, even though much may be asked of us.

Pause for silent reflection.

Second Reader: Luke 6:27–36

Response: Psalm 34

Side 1: I will bless the Lord at all times; his praise shall continually be in my mouth. My soul makes its boast in the Lord; let the humble hear and be glad. O magnify the Lord with me, and let us exalt his name together.

Side 2: I sought the Lord, and he answered me, and delivered me from all my fears. Look to him and be radiant; so your faces shall never be ashamed. This poor soul cried, and was heard by the Lord, and was saved from every trouble.

Side 1: The angel of the Lord encamps around those who fear him and delivers them. O taste and see that the Lord is good; happy are those who take refuge in him.
Side 2: O fear the Lord, you his holy ones, for those who fear him have no want. The young lions suffer want and hunger, but those who seek the Lord lack no good thing.

Side 1: Come, O children, listen to me; I will teach you the fear of the Lord. Which of you desires life and covets many days to enjoy good?
Side 2: Keep your tongue from evil and your lips from speaking deceit. Depart from evil and do good; seek peace and pursue it.

Side 1: The eyes of the Lord are on the righteous, and his ears are open to their cry. The face of the Lord is against evildoers, to cut off the remembrance of them from the earth.
Side 2: When the righteous cry for help, the Lord hears, and rescues them from all their troubles. The Lord is near to the brokenhearted and saves the crushed in spirit.

Side 1: Many are the afflictions of the righteous, but the Lord rescues them from them all. He keeps all their bones; not one of them will be broken. The Lord redeems the life of his servants.

Leader: With confidence in God, these women who served in El Salvador shared laughter and tears with the people whose daily lives were a struggle for justice. With confidence in God, we too ask for the grace to see goodness in the people whose needs call out to us.

All: God of the poor and the oppressed, whose love and care calls out to us and whose grace is enough to sustain us, lead us to your children who cry out for freedom and dignity.

Give us the courage to stand with the persecuted, believing that you hear their cry.

Pause for silent reflection.

Closing Song: "How Can I Keep from Singing" by Robert Lowry

Praying With Mary All Through the Year

Suggestion for atmosphere: Create a "Mary shrine" with statue, flowers, rosary, pictures of various apparitions; or if the parish has a grotto for Mary, outside or inside, gather there. Be sure to set up comfortable chairs.

Reader: Luke 1:39–46

At the point where the reading comes to the Magnificat, *invite the group to sing Mary's hymn of praise.*

Opening Song: "Holy Is His Name" by John Michael Talbot (Birdwing/Cherry Lane)

Leader: Welcome to this celebration of Mary, our mother. We are going to meet her today and allow her to show us the many things she can teach us when we are willing to walk with her and are careful to observe her.

GUIDED MEDITATION

Close your eyes. Slow down and deepen your breathing. Relax muscles in your head, neck, shoulders and limbs. Let go of intruding thoughts, current concerns. Simply be in the present moment and enter into visualizing the images to which you will be guided.

Instrumental music may be played softly in the background.

You are sitting in a garden with a calendar in your hands. Although flowers are blooming everywhere and the air is warm, you see that you have opened the calendar to December. Your memory fills with thoughts of all that December holds every year. While you are passing each memory through your mind, you look up, and standing a little distance away in the garden is a young, dark-haired woman who looks very pregnant. She smiles at you and offers you roses from the garden. Something about the image seems familiar. Glancing down at your calendar, you see December 12 in glowing light. Of course! The Virgin of Guadalupe has offered you her roses, and now she gently encourages you to help her give birth to Jesus in the world today.

Mary takes you by the hand. You are still clutching the calendar in the other. You walk with her into the bustling village of Bethlehem, crowded with visitors. As you walk together, looking for a room, the village grows into a large city. The housing is close together, traffic is dense, people are hurrying about. Some are in great need, but others don't notice. Mary tells you that Jesus is needed here, now. You feel her sense of urgency, and you want to be Jesus' hands and feet and heart. You notice that your calendar says December 25.

Mary is holding Jesus now and several dignified and stately men, dressed in the robes of a far Eastern culture, approach her. They offer gifts to her for the child. Mary ponders this gesture, while you ponder the ways of God who manifests the Son of God to all the world. A new year has begun with this epiphany!

A breeze turns your calendar page to February 11. You are in France, in the town of Lourdes. Mary is communicating with a young girl, and you listen as she encourages the girl to have faith. There is a running stream nearby and you are struck by the thought that living water is in this place.

The scene fades and you return to your garden. An unmistakable touch of spring is in the air. You look to where the pregnant lady of Guadalupe had beckoned to you with roses.

There she is again, but now an angel stands before her. Ah, this is how it all began, that pregnancy. Mary gives her *fiat*. It is March 25. What is God asking you to say yes to?

Springtime deepens and the garden reveals an empty tomb. Mary, with the ravaged look of a devastated mother, invites you to come to the tomb with her. She tells you how she has suffered the cruel loss of her Son. She pleads with you to keep his memory and message alive. She invites you to share her faith that he does still live.

Sleep overcomes you as the days grow warmer. A beautiful melody drifts through the air and gently wakens you. Mary is embracing another woman and singing for joy. It is her *Magnificat*. She praises God for God's blessings on the lowly. She prophecies an end to the suffering of the oppressed. May 31 is glowing on your calendar.

By now you understand that Mary permeates the calendar year. In every month she is honored for her faith, courage and love. You turn to June and there you find the Sacred Heart of Jesus and the Immaculate Heart of Mary, side by side. In July, Our Lady of Mt. Carmel graces the month. In August you meditate on her summons to heaven, and in September you celebrate her birthday.

Now the leaves are falling and the brisk October air blows through the remnants of your garden. An interesting scene unfolds before you. All the joys and sorrows of Mary, all the highlights of the life and ministry of Jesus are laid out in miniature scenes along the winding garden paths. Our Lady of the Rosary takes you by the hand and walks you through the mysteries.

At the end of the path, you arrive at the beginning of November. All of heaven comes to earth and you are joined by all the saints, as their queen takes her place at their head. Singing and rejoicing, the festive group continues to celebrate until a gradual hush moves over the crowd.

Mary stands apart and a light brighter than all the rest surrounds her. "I am the Immaculate Conception," she says. Your calendar has moved to December 8.

It's time to leave your garden, but you are filled with peace and gratitude. Mary has walked you through her story and you know she will always be with you every day of the year. Thank her, and ask her to keep you close to her Son. When you feel ready to leave the garden, open your eyes.

Reader: John 19:17–18, 25–27

Response: Psalm 91:1–7, 9–12, 14–16

Side 1: You who live in the shelter of the Most High, who abide in the shadow of the Almighty, will say to the Lord, "My refuge and my fortress; my God, in whom I trust."

Side 2: For he will deliver you from the snare of the fowler and from the deadly pestilence; he will cover you with his pinions, and under his wings you will find refuge; his faithfulness is a shield and buckler.

Side 1: You will not fear the terror of the night, or the arrow that flies by day, or the pestilence that stalks in darkness, or the destruction that wastes at noonday.

Side 2: A thousand may fall at your side, ten thousand at your right hand, but it will not come near you. Because you have made the Lord your refuge, the Most High your dwelling place, no evil shall befall you, no scourge come near your tent.

Side 1: For he will command his angels concerning you to guard you in all your ways. On their hands they will bear you up, so that you will not dash your foot against a stone.

Side 2: Those who love me, I will deliver; I will protect those who know my name.

Side 1: When they call to me, I will answer them; I will be with them in trouble, I will rescue them and honor them.

Side 2: With long life I will satisfy them and show them my salvation.

Leader: Jesus has given us his mother to teach and guide us. With her protection, we need not fear the twists and turns of life's journey. With confidence we pray:

Optional: *Play "Ave Maria, Ave" by Liam Lawton (GIA) from the album* In the Quiet. *This is a prayer that Mary guide us on our journey.*

All: We look to you, mother, as the one who models for us a gentle, strong acquiescence to the will of God. Please keep us faithful, as you were faithful, trusting in God's love throughout our lives. Amen.

Closing Song: "Hail Mary: Gentle Woman" by Carey Landry (OCP)

PART IV

✠

Prayer Services for
Religious Education Programs

Prayer to Bless Catechists
(at the beginning of the school year)

Suggestion for atmosphere: a table in the front of the room holding a candle for each catechist, the commissioning certificates and/or small gifts (such as a pin, a teaching resource or a book of prayers)

Opening Song: "We are the Light of the World" by Jean Anthony Grief (OCP)

During the singing, have catechists come forward to receive a lighted candle and carry it to their seat.

Leader: We welcome you, our catechists, here today to receive a blessing for the work you have agreed to undertake. We are grateful to you for your generous and selfless commitment of time, energy, talent and patience. We promise to support you with our prayers and assistance. Parents entrust their children to your guidance; the church entrusts its teaching mission to you; God calls you and fills you with the Spirit's inspiration.

Let us listen to an exhortation from Saint Peter:

First Reader: 1 Peter 5:1–7

Response: Psalm 145

Side 1: I will extol you, my God and King, and bless your name forever and ever. Every day I will bless you, and praise your name forever and ever.

Side 2: Great is the Lord, and greatly to be praised; his greatness is unsearchable. One generation shall laud your works to another, and shall declare your mighty acts.

Side 1: On the glorious splendor of your majesty, and on your wondrous works, I will meditate. The might of your awesome deeds shall be proclaimed, and I will declare your greatness.

Side 2: They shall celebrate the fame of your abundant goodness, and shall sing aloud of your righteousness. The Lord is gracious and merciful, slow to anger and abounding in steadfast love.

Side 1: The Lord is good to all, and his compassion is over all that he has made. All your works shall give thanks to you, O Lord, and all your faithful shall bless you.

Side 2: They shall speak of the glory of your kingdom, and tell of your power, to make known to all people your mighty deeds, and the glorious splendor of your kingdom.

Side 1: Your kingdom is an everlasting kingdom, and your dominion endures throughout all generations. The Lord is faithful in all his words, and gracious in all his deeds.

Side 2: The Lord upholds all who are falling, and raises up all who are bowed down. The eyes of all look to you, and you give them their food in due season.

Side 1: You open your hand, satisfying the desire of every living thing. The Lord is just in all his ways, and kind in all his doings.

Side 2: The Lord is near to all who call on him, to all who call on him in truth. He fulfills the desire of all who fear him; he also hears their cry, and saves them.

Side 1: The Lord watches over all who love him, but all the wicked he will destroy.

Side 2: My mouth will speak the praise of the Lord, and all flesh will bless his holy name forever and ever.

Leader: In our second reading, from the Letter to the Colossians, probably written by a disciple of Saint Paul, we will hear another exhortation to God's chosen ones. Realizing that catechists are specially chosen by God for their important task, let us be attentive to these words.

Second Reader: Colossians 3:12–17

REFLECTION

Leader: "Teach, in all wisdom," says Saint Paul. Teaching is a holy calling. You may wonder why you have entered into this adventure, committing your time and your energy to meetings, lesson plans and classroom encounters. You might be having doubts about your abilities, your effectiveness or your patience. You are probably excited, curious about the new year, maybe a little nervous. If you are wondering why you are doing this again, or for the first time, look within. Something in you has been tapped. You have heard the call and you have said, "Yes!"

Jesus was called "Rabbi," meaning *teacher*, and as a model for all catechists, he will show you how to do your job. When we look at Jesus as a teacher, we see a man in touch with his message and urgent about delivering it. He knew what he wanted to convey, and he went about the task consistently and tirelessly. Jesus had views about God and about the kingdom that he wanted to share. It was so important to him that people understand God as caring, loving and approachable. The kingdom was at hand, and people could help bring heaven on earth if they would love one another.

What message are you passionate about? What Christian ideals guide your life? Let that permeate your teaching.

Jesus had the wisdom to put profound teachings into simple forms. He touched people where they were, communicating through their daily experiences and at their level of understanding. His use of stories provided familiar settings through which he could make a point, provide food for thought, highlight a truth.

Are you in touch with the lives of your students? Do you reach them through their experiences? Teach the profound truths of our faith through examples they can understand.

Jesus taught the same things again and again in different kinds of ways. When he wanted to emphasize that God seeks out the lost and rejoices over finding them, he used a sheep image for shepherds, a coin image for householders and a runaway child for parents.

What same kinds of messages are repeated in your lessons? How much variety can you implement when repeating a concept? Be a creative lesson planner.

Jesus lived what he taught. While trying to open people's minds to accepting others who were different from them, Jesus himself reached out to non-Jews, to the alienated and outcast, to the labeled and the shunned. While teaching people to be liberated by the spirit of the law rather than enslaved by the letter of the law, he himself did the work of healing on the Sabbath.

Do you live the message you will be teaching? How will you model gospel values to your students? Be what you are asked to teach.

Indeed, you have been called, and teaching is a holy calling!

Invite the catechists to stand and to read their commitment.

Catechists: We ask our God, who chooses us for the task of teaching, to clothe us with compassion, kindness, humility, meekness, patience. We ask God to clothe us with love and to let peace rule our hearts. Prepared in this way, we commit ourselves to teach as Jesus did: to be urgent about our message, to reach the children at their level of experience, to clarify concepts creatively and to live the message we are teaching. We call on the Spirit of God to strengthen us in this commitment.

Call each catechist forward to receive a certificate and/or gift. When all have received, extend the blessing.

Leader: May God strengthen you for the work to which you have been called.

May Christ's word dwell in you, readily accessible to share with your students.

May the Holy Spirit put a song in your heart as you prepare the lessons you will teach.

May you be an earthen vessel to hold the treasure that is Jesus, so that the Lord's goodness will shine through all you do. Amen.

Closing Song: "Earthen Vessels" by John Foley, S.J. (OCP)

Prayer for a Catechist In-Service Meeting

Suggestion for atmosphere: *a prayer space that can be darkened for the quiet, guided imagery experience.*

Opening Song: "Be Not Afraid" by Bob Dufford, s.j. (OCP) *Answer When I Call* [handwritten]

Leader: Sometimes we might feel frightened by the task we have undertaken, or discouraged, or stressed. But it is good to step back from the work occasionally to recognize grace, to re-encounter the Holy One for whom we do this work and to assess how we can be doing it better. Our purpose for this meeting is to do that. So let us begin with a reading from the First Letter to the Corinthians.

Reader: 1 Corinthians 3:10–23

Response: Psalm 90:17

Leader: All belong to you, and you belong to Christ, and Christ belongs to God.
All: Let the favor of the Lord our God be upon us, and prosper for us the work of our hands.

Leader: You are laying a foundation that someone else will build on.
All: Let the favor of the Lord our God be upon us, and prosper for us the work of our hands.

Leader: Choose with care how you will build on the foundation that is Jesus Christ.
All: Let the favor of the Lord our God be upon us, and prosper for us the work of our hands.

Leader: If what has been built on the foundation survives, you will receive a reward.
All: Let the favor of the Lord our God be upon us, and prosper for us the work of our hands.

Leader: You are God's temple and God's Spirit dwells in you.
All: Let the favor of the Lord our God be upon us, and prosper for us the work of our hands.

Leader: Become fools in the eyes of the world that you may become wise in God.
All: Let the favor of the Lord our God be upon us, and prosper for us the work of our hands.

Leader: All things are yours, and you belong to Christ, and Christ belongs to God.
All: Let the favor of the Lord our God be upon us, and prosper for us the work of our hands.

Darken the room and lead the guided imagery experience.

GUIDED MEDITATION

Leader: Close your eyes. Slow down and deepen your breathing. Relax muscles in your head, neck, shoulders and limbs. Let go of intruding thoughts, current concerns. Simply be in the present moment and enter into visualizing the images to which you will be guided.

Instrumental music may be played softly in the background.

Imagine yourself sitting in the place where you usually prepare the lessons for your class. Is it quiet? Are there distractions, interruptions? Are your resources easily available? Now transport yourself to your ideal image of a planning space. What does it look like? How does it feel? Relax in this place and wait for the creative ideas to flow.

While you are thinking and planning, be aware that Jesus has entered the space. He is watching you with a twinkle in his eye, and a big smile forms on his face. He looks around at the ideal lesson-planning area you have imagined for yourself. He checks out your resources. What are you feeling as you watch him do this?

Still smiling, Jesus walks over to you and places his hand on yours. "Come with me," he beckons. He leads you to the edge of your space and, with a sweep of his arm, he gestures to the universe. The cosmos opens to you in all its splendor: sun, moon, stars, planets, solar systems. "I am the Christ of the cosmos," he says. "Open yourself to my mysteries."

Then he gestures again and a parade of people passes before you. Many races and nations, young and old, healthy and feeble, happy and sad, well fed and destitute. "I am the Savior of the world," he says. "Open yourself to my people."

Now Jesus leads you to a table where many newspapers are spread out. He invites you to read the headlines. There are tragic announcements of painful incidents around the world and in the local neighborhood. "I am Christ Crucified," says Jesus. "Open yourself to my pain."

Jesus tells you to remain at the table, and he turns the pages of the newspapers, directing your reading to the smaller headlines and the almost hidden stories. You read about Good Samaritans, charitable organizations, breakthroughs in medical treatments, peacemakers. "I am the Resurrected Christ," says Jesus. "Open yourself to my life."

Then Jesus invites you to kneel as he kneels beside you. A deep quiet descends over you. "Go within," he whispers. The quiet continues. A bright light enfolds you and you feel a penetrating warmth. "I am with you always," Jesus promises. "Open yourself to my Spirit."

When you look up, Jesus is gone from view, but you know he isn't really gone. You stand up and return to your lesson planning space. It looks different somehow. The essentials have changed, and you are feeling more peaceful about the task of preparation.

The varied images of Christ accompany you as you enter into plans for your next lesson.

This scene will slowly fade. When you are ready, open your eyes.

Invite the catechists to spend some time sharing what they were seeing or feeling during this experience and to talk to each other about how, where and when they plan their lessons. Then continue with the in-service agenda.

Leader: Ephesians 3:14–19

All: Now to him who by the power at work within us is able to accomplish abundantly far more than all we can ask or imagine, to him be glory in the church and in Christ Jesus to all generations, forever and ever. Amen.

Closing Song: "I Will Choose Christ" by Tom Booth (OCP)

Prayer to Bless Students

Suggestion for atmosphere: This blessing could be done in the church or other large gathering place where parents are also present, or it could be done in individual classrooms with teachers blessing their own students.

Opening Song: "You Have Called Us" (verses 1, 2 and 3) by Bernadette Farrell (OCP)

Teacher Leader: Welcome, children, to a new year of religion classes. We want to begin our year by asking Jesus to bless us. First, let us listen to what Jesus said about children.

Child Reader: Mark 10:13–16

Teacher Leader: Jesus, you called children to you and blessed them. We gather our children in your presence today to ask your blessing on them too. Children, respond to each prayer with "Bless us, Jesus." Jesus, keep our children safe from harm.
Children: Bless us, Jesus.

Teacher Leader: Jesus, teach our children to be kind.
Children: Bless us, Jesus.

Teacher Leader: Jesus, fill our children with your peace.
Children: Bless us, Jesus.

Teacher Leader: Jesus, teach our children how to pray.
Children: Bless us, Jesus.

Teacher Leader: Jesus, show our children how to love.
Children: Bless us, Jesus.

Child Leader: Children, respond to each prayer with "Bless our teachers, Jesus." With all the gentle caring of a friend,
Children: Bless our teachers, Jesus.

Child Leader: With patience, wisdom and good humor,
Children: Bless our teachers, Jesus.

Child Leader: With an understanding heart and open mind,
Children: Bless our teachers, Jesus.

Child Leader: With creativity and storytelling skills,
Children: Bless our teachers, Jesus.

Child Leader: With great love for following your way,
Children: Bless our teachers, Jesus.

Teacher Leader: Children, respond to each prayer with "Bless our families, Jesus." That our homes may nurture gospel values,
Children: Bless our families, Jesus.

Teacher Leader: That our homes may be the nest for building character,
Children: Bless our families, Jesus.

Teacher Leader: That our homes may be safe havens from violence,
Children: Bless our families, Jesus.

Teacher Leader: That our homes may plant the seeds for future growth,
Children: Bless our families, Jesus.

Teacher Leader: That our homes may provide the building blocks of peace,
Children: Bless our families, Jesus.

Child Leader: Children, respond to each prayer with "Jesus, bless us all." We turn to you in joy and sadness.

Children: Jesus, bless us all.

Child Leader: We call on you for strength and guidance.
Children: Jesus, bless us all.

Child Leader: We look for you in truth and goodness.
Children: Jesus, bless us all.

Child Leader: We bring to you our hope and wonder.
Children: Jesus, bless us all.

Child Leader: We walk with you in faith and love.
Children: Jesus, bless us all.

Teacher Leader: Children, with these blessings we are ready to begin our year together. May you grow and be happy and know that Jesus is always with you. Let us sing together.

Closing Song: "You Have Called Us" (verses 4 and 5) by Bernadette Farrell (OCP)

Prayer With Children in Elementary Level Classes

Suggestion for atmosphere: *Take the children to the prayer space in the classroom or create one by moving the desks around. Indicate that this is a special prayer time by transforming the space in some significant way. Use a picture or statue of Jesus, pictures of the students and pictures of children around the world.*

Opening Song: "Father of Peace" by Michael Lynch (Raven Music)

Teacher: Jesus wanted people to know that God is like our parents—someone who loves us, forgives us when we make a mistake, gives us the things we need, takes care of us when we are sick. Jesus taught people to call God their Father when they pray. Here is what he said:

Reader: Matthew 6:7–15

Teacher: Do you recognize those words of Jesus? We call this the Our Father. Let's pray that prayer together now.

Lead children in praying the Our Father as they all hold hands.

Teacher: Jesus was a good teacher and he loved children. He is with us in our classroom today, and he goes with us wherever we are. Let's talk to him right now. When I point to you after each thing I say to Jesus, you say, "Jesus, bless us." Let us call on Jesus to be with us in our classroom today. Jesus, we are the children who come to you wanting to learn.
Children: Jesus, bless us.

Teacher: Jesus, we are the children who learn from you how to love.
Children: Jesus, bless us.

Teacher: Jesus, we are the children who make mistakes but want to grow
Children: Jesus, bless us.

Teacher: Jesus, we are the children who smile and laugh and play and make friends.
Children: Jesus, bless us.

Teacher: Jesus, we are the children who cry and get hurt and are sometimes sad.
Children: Jesus, bless us.

Teacher: Jesus, we are the children who want to do our very best every day.
Children: Jesus, bless us.

Teacher: Jesus, we know you are a friend we can always talk to. It is so wonderful to know you care about us. We believe that you see inside our hearts and you know what is in our thoughts. Thank you for being so close.
Children: Amen.

Teacher: Now let us pray for other children. After each prayer I say to Jesus, you say, "Jesus, bless them." Jesus, we remember the children who go to bed hungry at night.
Children: Jesus, bless them.

Teacher: Jesus, we remember the children who are afraid of the bombs and gunshots they hear.
Children: Jesus, bless them.

Teacher: Jesus, we remember the children who lost their mothers and fathers in a war.
Children: Jesus, bless them.

Teacher: Jesus, we remember the children who are too sick to play with their friends.
Children: Jesus, bless them.

Teacher: Jesus, we remember the children who have nothing to wear.
Children: Jesus, bless them.

Teacher: Jesus, we remember the children who work hard in fields and factories and can't go to school.
Children: Jesus, bless them.

Teacher: Jesus, there are many children who are hurting in our world today. We know you love all children. Let children everywhere feel your love when they are afraid or lonely or in pain. Help us to notice when someone is hurting. Teach us to be kind and gentle and to share whatever we have.
Children: Amen.

Teacher: Another time Jesus told people they should be like lights to light up the world by going out and doing good things. Here is what he said.

Reader: Matthew 5:14–16

Teacher: Today you prayed for other children, not just for yourselves. That's a good thing. Let's end our prayer by singing about how we will light up our world just as Jesus wants us to do.

Closing Song: "This Little Light of Mine"

Prayer to Bless Parents

Suggestion for atmosphere: Use this prayer at a parent meeting at the beginning of a school year or any time during the year. You will need a cassette or CD player for instrumental music during the quiet reflection time and hymnals for the opening and closing songs.

Opening Song: "On Eagle's Wings" (all verses, especially 1 and 4) by Michael Joncas (OCP)

Leader: Welcome, parents. Today we call on God to bless you in your role of parenting and to strengthen you to meet the challenges of that role. Let us continue this blessing time by listening to a segment from the Letter to the Ephesians, which gives recommendations for the Christian household.

Reader: Ephesians 5:21—6:3, 10, 14–18

Response: Sirach 18:1–14

Side 1: He who lives forever created the whole universe; the Lord alone is just. To none has he given power to proclaim his works; and who can search out his mighty deeds?

Side 2: Who can measure his majestic power? And who can fully recount his mercies? It is not possible to diminish or increase them, nor is it possible to fathom the wonders of the Lord.

Side 1: When human beings have finished, they are just beginning, and when they stop, they are still perplexed. What are human beings and of what use are they? What is good in them, and what is evil?

Side 2: The number of days in their life is great if they reach one hundred years. Like a drop of water from the sea and a grain of sand, so are a few years among the days of eternity.

Side 1: That is why the Lord is patient with them and pours out his mercy upon them. He sees and recognizes that their end is miserable; therefore he grants them forgiveness all the more.

Side 2: The compassion of human beings is for their neighbors, but the compassion of the Lord is for every living thing. He rebukes and trains and teaches them, and turns them back, as a shepherd his flock.

Side 1: He has compassion on those who accept his discipline and who are eager for his precepts.

GUIDED MEDITATION

(Read by a parent or divided among several parents): What an awesome task to be called to be cocreators with God in giving life to our children! What a profound calling to be given the responsibility of nurturing and guiding our children in faith, in virtue, in character development! What trust God places in us by sharing the work of formation!

As we reflect today on the role of parenting, we can call to mind the many things this role calls forth from us: Our love must be patient, our understanding must be inspired; our discipline needs consistency, our skills need updating; our time must find availability, our speech must find the right words.

We love our children as God loves us, and so we know how much we care for their greater good. We know the meaning of sacrifice and the endless extent of our efforts to give our children what they need.

As parents we experience the pride of seeing little people who are embracing our values, speaking thoughts we have planted, expressing faith we have shared. We feel the joy of witnessing our efforts bearing fruit.

For those frustrating times when we don't immediately see rewarding results from our labors of love, let us ask God for patience and trust. We are not alone in the formation process—and God isn't finished yet, with us or with our children! For those glorious times when our children's goodness shines like stars, let us thank God for allowing us to be partners in the great venture of shaping lives. Let us bow in humility before the wondrous mystery of our call to be parents.

Let us pause to reflect.

After some quiet reflection time, play Liam Lawton's blessing for parents: "Blest Are You" from In the Quiet *(GIA). Ask parents to bow their heads to receive a blessing.*

Leader: Compassionate God, our refuge and our strength, bless us with the joys of family love and caring. Bless these parents with patience and understanding. Bless them with courage and consistency in their discipline. Bless them with the gift of time for their children. Bless them with faith in the partnership they share with you.

Parents: Partner God, thank you for inviting us to be cocreators. Our children are precious gifts, entrusted to us for upbringing, and we are humbly in awe of that trust. Help us to nurture the faith you plant in them. Be with us to guide us in our parenting. Protect our children from the mistakes we sometimes make. We welcome you always to our family table and into our daily living. May we remain aware of the many ways you touch our lives forever. Amen.

Closing Song: "Table of Plenty" (especially verses 3 and 4) by Dan Schutte (OCP)

Prayer with High School Classes

Suggestion for atmosphere: Meet in a room that can be darkened for the guided imagery experience. Have instrumental music ready to play and comfortable chairs.

Opening Song: "Be With Me, Lord" by Tom Booth (OCP)

Leader: Tonight our prayer will lead us to a "Jesus encounter." To prepare for this, let us listen to a story, from the Gospel of John, about a man who sought his own encounter with Jesus. It was risky for him to do this because he belonged to a group of Pharisees who didn't approve of Jesus.

Reader: John 3:1–16

Leader: Real friends are the people who give us good advice. Jesus was a friend to Nicodemus. Friends can be found outside our own group. Nicodemus was open to making that discovery.

In the wisdom literature of the Old Testament there is good advice regarding friendship. Let us read an example from the book of Sirach (6:5–10, 14–17).

Side 1: Pleasant speech multiplies friends, and a gracious tongue multiplies courtesies.
Side 2: Let those who are friendly with you be many, but let your advisers be one in a thousand.

Side 1: When you gain friends, gain them through testing and do not trust them hastily.
Side 2: For there are friends who are such when it suits them, but they will not stand by you in time of trouble.

Side 1: And there are friends who change into enemies and tell of the quarrel to your disgrace.
Side 2: And there are friends who sit at your table, but they will not stand by you in time of trouble.

Side 1: Faithful friends are a sturdy shelter; whoever finds one has found a treasure.
Side 2: Faithful friends are beyond price; no amount can balance their worth.

Side 1: Faithful friends are life-saving medicine; and those who fear the Lord will find them.
Side 2: Those who fear the Lord direct their friendship aright, for as they are, so are their neighbors also.

Leader: Jesus is a faithful friend we can always count on. Tonight we are going to meet this friend through someone who will lead us to him. To prepare for this, close your eyes. Slow down and deepen your breathing. Relax the muscles in your head, neck, shoulders and limbs. Let go of intruding thoughts, current concerns. Simply be in the present moment and enter into visualizing the images to which you will be guided.

GUIDED MEDITATION

It is nighttime. You are outside, and there is darkness all around you. You hear crickets, an owl, a distant splash, but mostly you hear silence. It is a clear night and the stars are everywhere overhead. You sit down in very soft grass, then lean back to contemplate the sky. How mysterious the distant planets and the stars! Caught up in wonder, you begin to touch the other mysteries in your life: relationships, your place in the world, your future, your connection to all that lives.

Feel your questions formulating. What would you like to ask God if you could meet God face to face?

As your eyes adjust to the darkness, you see a person coming toward you. He offers a friendly greeting and identifies himself as Nicodemus. You invite him to sit beside you on the grass. Nicodemus tells you that this quiet, beautiful night reminds him of a night long ago when he went looking for Jesus. He wanted Jesus to answer questions about the mysteries of life that he was pondering. He assures you that Jesus is a good listener with wise answers, and he asks you to take a walk with him.

Getting up, you walk with Nicodemus toward the sound of the distant water. The occasional splash grows louder. Following a path around a large wall of rock, you come to a place where the moon illuminates the shiny surface of a flowing stream. The water tumbles over rocks as it moves. A frog or a fish makes sudden, occasional movements; otherwise there is only the flowing water.

Nicodemus stops at the water's edge and asks you to watch the movement. "There is mystery here; contemplate it," he says.

The water moves around obstacles. It doesn't stop. It goes forward gently. It helps what is stuck to get unstuck. It is filled with life. It shares its life. Its origins and its destiny are not visible; only its current course in this place and moment can be seen, illuminated by the night.

Nicodemus tells you that he asked Jesus how to be born again. It was a night like this. Jesus told him he had to be born of water and the Spirit. "I didn't understand," says Nicodemus, "until I looked into the stream. I'm going to leave you now, but you won't be alone."

Nicodemus walks away into the darkness. Jesus steps out of the shadows. He doesn't say a word, but gestures toward the stream. You are perfectly comfortable in his presence as you watch the flowing water and absorb its mystery. What do you see? What do you hear? What are you feeling? What do you want to ask Jesus?

Jesus stays there in the quiet with you for a while, answering your questions and asking some. What does he suggest about your life? What advice does he give about living with mystery? What does he share from his own life experiences? What does he seem to know best about you?

It has been a long night. A faint glow on the horizon tells you dawn is coming. Express your gratitude to Jesus for his friendship, wisdom and guidance. He stays by the stream when you get up to leave. Somehow you know you will find him there whenever you return, and that comforts you.

When you feel ready, open your eyes.

Optional: If students are accustomed to journaling, ask them to spend a little time writing about this experience in their journals. Or discuss the experience with a few leading questions: Were you comfortable with Nicodemus? With Jesus? What did the water teach you? How would a daytime encounter be different from this nighttime experience? Would you ever use this form of meditation again when you want to talk to Jesus? End the discussion or reflective writing time with the following prayers:

Reader: Philippians 1:9–11

All: Jesus, friend and teacher, walk with us in the light of day and talk with us in the quiet night. Keep us attentive to the many ways through which you come and the many signs through which you speak. May we trust your friendship and learn from you how to be faithful friends to others. We reverence our Creator God and give praise through you and with you. Amen.

Closing Song: "Awesome God" by Rich Mullins/Tom Booth (BMG Songs, Inc.)

Prayer for an Adult Faith-Formation Gathering

Suggestion for atmosphere: Adults on a spiritual journey are generally experiencing a longing for something. Life has given them many experiences and they want to connect those to their faith journey. In this prayer, the music is particularly important for creating the atmosphere of openness and longing that characterize the adult need to keep learning and growing.

Opening Song: "Open My Eyes" by Jesse Manibusan (OCP)

Sit in silence for a few minutes after the song. The musician(s) could continue to play, and then taper off.

First Reader: 1 John 4:6–10

Psalm Response: Psalm 138

All: I give you thanks, O Lord, with my whole heart.

Leader: I bow down toward your holy temple and give thanks to your name for your steadfast love and your faithfulness; for you have exalted your name and your word above everything.
All: I give you thanks, O Lord, with my whole heart.

Leader: On the day I called, you answered me, you increased my strength of soul. All the kings of the earth shall praise you, O Lord, for they have heard the words of your mouth.
All: I give you thanks, O Lord, with my whole heart.

Leader: They shall sing of the ways of the Lord, for great is the glory of the Lord. For though the Lord is high, he regards the lowly; but the haughty he perceives from far away.

All: I give you thanks, O Lord, with my whole heart.

Leader: Though I walk in the midst of trouble, you preserve me against the wrath of my enemies; you stretch out your hand, and your right hand delivers me.
All: I give you thanks, O Lord, with my whole heart.

Leader: The Lord will fulfill his purpose for me; your steadfast love, O Lord, endures forever. Do not forsake the work of your hands.
All: I give you thanks, O Lord, with my whole heart.

Second Reader:

We act sometimes as though we could teach ourselves, knowing in advance where and when and how God will make his presence known to us.

We profess that we believe God to be everywhere, but we act sometimes as though we really think that God is to be found primarily, if not exclusively, at times and places that are specifically marked "Sacred. God present here!"

But God is not bound by our limitations. He is not restricted to the Sabbath's dawn, to 11 A.M. on Sundays and 8 P.M. on Wednesdays, or to the buildings we have set aside for God. God is where we are. And where we are not. All the time. No exceptions. We can expect to be surprised by God.[4]

Response: Psalm 139:1–18, 23–24

Side 1: O Lord, you have searched me and known me. You know when I sit down and when I rise up; you discern my thoughts from far away.
Side 2: You search out my path and my lying down, and are acquainted with all my ways. Even before a word is on my tongue, O Lord, you know it completely.

Side 1: You hem me in, behind and before, and lay your hand upon me. Such knowledge is too wonderful for me; it is so high that I cannot attain it.

Side 2: Where can I go from your spirit? Or where can I flee from your presence? If I ascend to heaven, you are there; if I make my bed in Sheol, you are there.

Side 1: If I take the wings of the morning and settle at the farthest limits of the sea, even there your hand shall lead me, and your right hand shall hold me fast.

Side 2: If I say, "Surely the darkness shall cover me, and the light around me become night," even the darkness is not dark to you; the night is as bright as the day; for darkness is as light to you.

Side 1: For it was you who formed my inward parts; you knit me together in my mother's womb.

Side 2: I praise you, for I am fearfully and wonderfully made. Wonderful are your works; that I know very well.

Side 1: My frame was not hidden from you, when I was being made in secret, intricately woven in the depths of the earth.

Side 2: Your eyes beheld my unformed substance. In your book were written all the days that were formed for me, when none of them as yet existed.

Side 1: How weighty to me are your thoughts, O God! How vast is the sum of them! I try to count them—they are more than the sand; I come to the end—I am still with you.

Side 2: Search me, O God, and know my heart; test me and know my thoughts. See if there is any wicked way in me, and lead me in the way everlasting.

Third Reader: Ephesians 1:17–19

All: We too pray, O God, that you will give us wisdom and enlighten our hearts. You, who have no limitations, surprise us with your presence and your grace. Call us to hope and to love.

Transform us by your power that we may be mystics and saints. We long for you, God. Amen.

Observe a few minutes of silence.

Closing Song: "There Is a Longing" by Anne Quigley (OCP)

PART V

✠

Prayer Services for Parish Groups

A Prayer for the Parish Staff

Suggestion for atmosphere: A parish staff meeting can be conducted within the context of this prayer setting. Arrange comfortable seating and place the Bible and a lighted candle in a prominent position.

Opening Song: "Only This I Want" by Dan Schutte (OCP)

Leader: Let us bring our concerns for our parish to prayer.

All: In a spirit of collaboration we envision what our people need from us. Bring our vision in line with yours, Lord God of all the people. Open our ears that we may hear their needs and your solutions. Open our eyes that we may see their concerns and your touch. Open our hearts that we may welcome their input and your inspiration.

Reading: Sirach 4:11–18

Response: Psalm 98

Side 1: O sing to the Lord a new song, for he has done marvelous things. His right hand and his holy arm have gotten him victory.
Side 2: The Lord has made known his victory; he has revealed his vindication in the sight of the nations.

Side 1: He has remembered his steadfast love and faithfulness to the house of Israel. All the ends of the earth have seen the victory of our God.
Side 2: Make a joyful noise to the Lord, all the earth; break forth into joyous song and sing praises.

Side 1: Sing praises to the Lord with the lyre, with the lyre and the sound of melody. With trumpets and the sound of the horn make a joyful noise before the King, the Lord.
Side 2: Let the sea roar, and all that fills it; the world and those who live in it.

Side 1: Let the floods clap their hands; let the hills sing together for joy at the presence of the Lord, for he is coming to judge the earth.
Side 2: He will judge the world with righteousness, and the peoples with equity.

Leader: In the silence that follows, let us prepare ourselves to receive some questions that could guide our sharing and planning today.

Pause for silent prayer.

Leader: I invite you to sit for a while with each question. Hold in your heart whatever ideas come to you as the questions flow. We will share our ideas after all the questions are offered.

Adapt the questions to the particular purpose of your parish staff meeting. Allow a pause for reflection after each one.

What are the most pressing needs in our parish at this time? What is happening in our parish that can be celebrated? Where have we failed to address any concerns? Who are the people who have touched us most significantly? Who have we touched and where is the evidence? How are we teaching and healing as Jesus did? Why are we engaged in the particular plans and projects that are currently consuming our time, finances and resources?

As we now address the who, what, where, why and how of our parish ministry, let us listen carefully to the Spirit and to each other.

Repeat each question now, following each with discussion time. Allow the meeting agenda to flow from the shared responses. When the business of the meeting has been sufficiently covered, conclude with the prayers that follow.

Leader: Let us pray. (*Read Ephesians 3:14–19.*)

All: Bless the work of our hands, Lord, and guide our parish. Give us a common heart and unity of purpose; and may all we do be done according to your will. Amen.

Closing Song: "One Bread, One Body" by John Foley, S.J. (OCP)

A Prayer for the Parish Council

Suggestion for atmosphere: *This prayer can be used with any parish council meeting, but especially during a goal-setting meeting early in the year or at the time of a mid-year evaluation.*

Opening Song: "We Are Many Parts" by Marty Haugen (GIA)

Leader: We are here tonight to plan (or evaluate) the direction of our parish council work. Let us prepare for this by focusing on what the prophet Micah said about what God wants us to do.

Reader: Micah 6:6–8

Leader: Through the prophet Micah, God asked people to do what is right. To the following petitions, please respond: "Lord, hear our prayer."

Reader: That we may act in the name of justice when injustice hurts the poor.
All: Lord, hear our prayer.

Reader: That we may choose honesty over dishonesty in all our dealings with God's people.
All: Lord, hear our prayer.

Reader: That we may do good things with our time, money and abilities.
All: Lord, hear our prayer.

Reader: That we may not profit at the expense of those less fortunate.
All: Lord, hear our prayer.

Reader: That we may not engage in violence in any form as we seek to make peace in our very disturbed society and world.
All: Lord, hear our prayer.

Leader: Through the prophet Micah, God asked people to love tenderly. To the following petitions, please respond, "Lord, hear our prayer."

Reader: That we may work for stability in our families and faithfulness in our relationships.
All: Lord, hear our prayer.

Reader: That we may be slow to anger and quick to forgive.
All: Lord, hear our prayer.

Reader: That we may care for children, the elderly, society's outcasts, the weak and the lost with the gentle tenderness of God's own love.
All: Lord, hear our prayer.

Reader: That we make no one our enemy, never seek revenge and always refrain from judgments.
All: Lord, hear our prayer.

Reader: That we may act in the name of love even when our efforts are misunderstood.
All: Lord, hear our prayer.

Leader: Through the prophet Micah, we are invited to walk humbly with God. To the following petitions, please respond, "Lord, hear our prayer."

Reader: That pride and arrogance may find no foothold in our hearts.
All: Lord, hear our prayer.

Reader: That we may nourish a prayer life that will keep us open to God's grace.
All: Lord, hear our prayer.

Reader: That we may value virtue and practice fidelity.
All: Lord, hear our prayer.

Reader: That our thoughts be turned to God so we may put on the mind of Christ.
All: Lord, hear our prayer.

Reader: That our footsteps may follow the Way, the Truth and the Life.
All: Lord, hear our prayer.

Leader: God of our ancestors, for many ages you have directed people to be humble, loving and good. As we look at our parish family and recognize its many gifts, let us be aware that you are working in and through all the goodness we see. May all we do be done in your name and for your glory and praise.

All: Amen.

FOR REFLECTION AND SHARING

Leader: What do you hope this council can be and do?

Discuss goals for the year (or evaluate goals already in place). Continue the business agenda.

CONCLUDING PRAYER

Reading: Philippians 2:2–4, 14–16

Response: Psalm 111

Side 1: Praise the Lord! I will give thanks to the Lord with my whole heart, in the company of the upright, in the congregation.
Side 2: Great are the works of the Lord, studied by all who delight in them. Full of honor and majesty is his work, and his righteousness endures forever.

Side 1: He has gained renown by his wonderful deeds; the Lord is gracious and merciful. He provides food for those who fear him; he is ever mindful of his covenant.
Side 2: He has shown his people the power of his works, in giving them the heritage of the nations.

Side 1: The works of his hands are faithful and just; all his precepts are trustworthy. They are established forever and ever, to be performed with faithfulness and uprightness.
Side 2: He sent redemption to his people; he has commanded his covenant forever. Holy and awesome is his name.

All: The fear of the Lord is the beginning of wisdom; all those who practice it have a good understanding. His praise endures forever.

Closing Song: "This Is" (Song of Micah) by Liam Lawton (GIA) or "What Is Our Service to Be" by Scot Crandal (OCP)

A Prayer for Liturgical Ministers

Suggestion for setting: A gathering in the church for the purpose of blessing all who are involved in liturgical ministry; this prayer service could be used before or after convening the group for a training session/meeting.

Opening Song: "River of Glory" by Dan Schutte (OCP)

Leader: We are grateful for being called to minister at the eucharistic assemblies of our parish community. We ask God to bless us in our various roles and to keep us always mindful of how we can enhance the community's experience of prayer and worship.

First Reader: Deuteronomy 7:6–9

Response: Psalm 149:1–6a

Reader: Praise the Lord! Sing to the Lord a new song, his praise in the assembly of the faithful. Let Israel be glad in its Maker; let the children of Zion rejoice in their King.
All: Sing "River of Glory" refrain

Reader: Let them praise his name with dancing, making melody to him with tambourine and lyre. For the Lord takes pleasure in his people; he adorns the humble with victory.
All: Sing "River of Glory" refrain

Reader: Let the faithful exult in glory; let them sing for joy on their couches. Let the high praises of God be in their throats. Praise the Lord!

All: Sing "River of Glory" refrain

REFLECTION

Second Reader: Your choice to serve places you in a unique position of importance in parish ministry. Since the Eucharist is central to our lives as Catholic Christians, anything we do to enhance the experience of liturgy for our community will help it to bond in Christ.

Hospitality ministers set the tone of welcome. How important it is for you to let people know they are wanted and will be comfortable!

The environment committee creates the climate for seasonal celebrations. How essential it is that you help participants in liturgy relate to a theme for their worship!

Musicians invite and engage the whole person, touching the heart and moving the spirit with music well chosen andled. How wonderful it is to make this offering of your God-given talent!

Lectors convey the presence of God through the power of the Word. How creatively that Word can open something new in us when you proclaim it well!

Servers at the altar assist the smooth function and flow of liturgy. How inspiring is your demeanor when you show reverence and attention!

Eucharistic ministers serve as hosts and hostesses, offering the sacred meal to those who bring their hunger. How special your smile of welcome and your words of faith!

Together, liturgical ministers invite and facilitate communal celebration. When offered as prayer, your time, effort and expertise will provide an inspiring atmosphere for worship. This is your gift to the Body of Christ, the church.

Pause to reflect.

Leader: As ministers we must put on the mind of the Christ we serve in one another. Saint Paul suggests to us a way to imitate the humility of Jesus.

First Reader: Philippians 2:4–11

All: Glory to you, Jesus Christ, crucified and risen and present to us through the Eucharist. We praise and bless you. We seek to imitate your spirit of giving. We bow our heads and bend our knees to you who are Lord and Savior. We ask your blessing on our ministry.

Leader: May God, who accepted the sacrifice of Jesus, prepare our minds and hearts to assist at the memorial of this sacrifice.

All: Amen.

Leader: May Jesus, who asked that we remember him when we gather to break bread and to break open the Word, teach us his ways.

All: Amen.

Leader: May the Spirit, who fills the hearts of all the faithful, make us holy and humble.

All: Amen.

Closing Song: "I Am the Bread of Life" by John Michael Talbot (Birdwing /Cherry Lane and BMG)

A Prayer for RCIA Leaders and Candidates/Catechumens

Suggestions for use: This prayer service can be used at the beginning of a new RCIA program or in its early stages. Any materials for study that are going to be given to the participants, including a Bible, can be given in a ceremony during this service. Prepare the prayer space with comfortable seating, music and Scripture, materials to be distributed.

Opening Song: "Strength for the Journey" by Michael John Poirier

Leader: God has called you into a covenant relationship from your birth because God has loved you from the beginning. Ezekiel describes the covenant in terms of ongoing conversion and God's untiring efforts to reach out to us.

Reader: Ezekiel 36:24–28

Response: Psalm 71:1–6, 15–23

Side 1: In you, O Lord, I take refuge; let me never be put to shame. In your righteousness deliver me and rescue me; incline your ear to me and save me.
Side 2: Be to me a rock of refuge, a strong fortress to save me, for you are my rock and my fortress. Rescue me, O my God, from the hand of the wicked, from the grasp of the unjust and cruel.

Side 1: For you, O Lord, are my hope, my trust, O Lord, from my youth. Upon you I have leaned from my birth; it was you who took me from my mother's womb. My praise is continually of you.
Side 2: My mouth will tell of your righteous acts, of your deeds of salvation all day long, though their number is past my knowledge.

Side 1: I will come praising the mighty deeds of the Lord God, I will praise your righteousness, yours alone.
Side 2: O God, from my youth you have taught me, and I still proclaim your wondrous deeds. So even to old age and gray hairs, O God, do not forsake me, until I proclaim your might to all the generations to come.

Side 1: Your power and your righteousness, O God, reach the high heavens. You who have done great things, O God, who is like you?
Side 2: You who have made me see many troubles and calamities will revive me again; from the depths of the earth you will bring me up again.

Side 1: You will increase my honor, and comfort me once again. I will also praise you with the harp for your faithfulness, O my God; I will sing praises to you with the lyre, O Holy One of Israel.
Side 2: My lips will shout for joy when I sing praises to you; my soul also, which you have rescued.

Leader: I would like to lead you on a journey in your imagination right now, so please relax and close your eyes. (*Instrumental music could be played softly in the background as the leader continues.*)

Slow down and deepen your breathing. Relax the muscles in your head, neck, shoulders, limbs. Let go of intruding thoughts, current concerns. Simply be in the present moment and enter into visualizing the images to which you will be guided.

Imagine you are in the place where you first desired to become a Catholic. Who is with you in this place? What would you like to say to this person or what do you want to ask of these people? If you are alone, what do you want to say to God?

Pause a moment for reflection.

Now imagine yourself in the future, with the RCIA program behind you. You are a Catholic. How do you see yourself being accepted and involved in your community of faith? What do you hope for yourself from this community?

Pause a moment for reflection.

Now bring yourself to the present. With your eyes still closed, you are aware of others in this room with you. Imagine their stories—the circumstances and people who may have brought them here. The hopes and dreams they have for their faith journies.

Pause a moment for reflection.

Sense the importance of your being together in this place at this time. You are the church in miniature, mirroring its beginnings. You will have teachers to guide you and Jesus to inspire you. You will have rituals to take part in and traditions to develop. You will receive a sacred trust to keep God's Word alive in your own heart and in the community. Imagine yourself joining hands with the people who share this sacred trust. Bow your head and spend some time in prayer.

Pause a moment for reflection.

When you are ready, open your eyes. We will now share a ritual of blessing each other.

Reader: 2 Peter 1:5–11

Leader and sponsors (*face the candidates and raise a hand in blessing over them*): May you support your faith with goodness, knowledge and self-control.
Candidates: Amen.

Leader and sponsors: May you endure in godliness with mutual affection and love.
Candidates: Amen.

Leader and sponsors: May you be eager to confirm your election and to enter the kingdom of Jesus Christ.
Candidates: Amen.

Distribute materials, Bibles, to the program participants.

Candidates (*face sponsors and raise a hand in blessing over them*): May God give you wisdom and gentleness for your role as faith companions.
Sponsors: Amen.

Candidates: May this be a time of deeply satisfying spiritual renewal of your own covenant relationship with God.
Sponsors: Amen.

Candidates: May you be effective and fruitful and never stumble.
Sponsors: Amen.

Closing Song: "Companions on the Journey" by Carey Landry (OCP)

A Prayer for Bereavement Groups

Suggestion for use: Prayer and sharing time in a grief support group; arrange chairs in a circle. or in several smaller circles if the group is large.

Opening Song: "Shepherd Me, O God" by Marty Haugen (GIA)

Leader: Grieving is a process, and there is no way to rush through it, to be over and done with it quickly. God is waiting to offer new life whenever we feel ready to receive it, but for a while we can't see anything clearly except our own pain.

During the time we need for feeling our loss, we ask God to bless us with the presence of people who will allow us to come to peace in our own time. People who just walk with us, listen to us, and maybe share the Scriptures with us. The disciples walking the road to Emmaus, after the death of Jesus, were blessed with that kind of presence.

Reader: Luke 24:13–35

Leader: They felt so lost, so shattered. They had nurtured a dream, and it had died. Their hopes were all wrapped up in a person—and he had died.

What do you do when death enters life and leaves you broken? Whether it is the death of a dream or the death of a person, or any other kind of loss, the brokenness is there.

The two disciples—the followers of a dream (for that's who they were)—were stunned by their loss. Their vision became so fixed on the loss that they were temporarily blind to the new life around them, the New Life walking beside them and speaking to their hearts.

Sadness needed its own time to be. Fresh insight and reclaimed joy would come with the breaking of bread. But that was still down the road a way. Meanwhile, there was a journey in sadness to make.

They were not alone on that journey.

Mercifully, we are not alone either when we walk the long road that leads us away from a scene of death. We might not immediately see or hear or understand, but comfort and wisdom and insight are being offered all around us—in the presence of a friend, the words of a stranger, the movement of a barely discernible Spirit within.

It takes time, but the road is long enough to give us the time we need. First, we realize that the dream or the person is gone. That's when hope fades, crushing defeat seems to suffocate us and despair is just around the corner. Then we start asking ourselves and other people what we are going to do without that dream or that love which sustained us.

It is when we ask the questions that the answers begin to come: not in a sudden rush of clarity, but slowly; not to the skeptics and cynics, but to the honest, soul-searching men and women whose pain of loss has left them vulnerable; not from an indefinable source, but from the comforting familiarity of Scripture and those people who interpret its treasures to us.

And while the road continues to be long, and the sadness still has not lifted, and the answers still remain unclear, there might come, even so, a ray of hope. However small, there might begin in us a spark that promises fuller light. We might even begin to suspect that the dream hasn't really died, just our limited interpretation of it. Or that the person we love isn't really dead, just our relationship has been transformed and our way of relating in the past can never be reclaimed.

The new reality might still be hard to accept. Dreams and persons in whom we have invested much life and love are deeply missed. But the black emptiness and hopelessness fade after that spark of new insight is lit.

When we get caught up in the answers and interpretations that are all around us, like the disciples on the way to Emmaus, we forget to grieve anymore. The journey of sadness comes to an end, and we are eager only for the new insights to remain with us as another day ends and darkness descends.

If we are willing to accept that there is more than one way of looking at tragedy, if we are honestly searching for a way to make sense out of suffering, if we can still open our hearts and homes to the people and experiences that life keeps bringing to us—then, like the disciples at Emmaus, our hearts will burn again with love and joy. There will be peace all around us, and we will know that the Lord is quietly calling us to live.

At the end of the reflection, allow a few minutes for silence. Then, in the continuing stillness, play the song "In the Quiet" by Liam Lawton. He wrote this song for the events of September 11, 2001, and it beautifully reflects the sentiments of the Emmaus story. It is on the album In the Quiet, *published by GIA.*

Leader: Take some time now to share with your group your own experiences of the kind of support you have needed and the kind of support you have received.

Allow time for sharing.

Leader: Calling on God to help us along the way of healing, let us pray Psalm 86:

Side 1: Incline your ear, O Lord, and answer me, for I am poor and needy. Preserve my life, for I am devoted to you; save your servant who trusts in you.

Side 2: You are my God; be gracious to me, O Lord, for to you do I cry all day long. Gladden the soul of your servant, for to you, O Lord, I lift up my soul.

Side 1: For you, O Lord, are good and forgiving, abounding in steadfast love to all who call on you.

Side 2: Give ear, O Lord, to my prayer; listen to my cry of supplication. In the day of my trouble I call on you, for you will answer me.

Side 1: There is none like you among the gods, O Lord, nor are there any works like yours. All the nations you have made shall come and bow down before you, O Lord, and shall glorify your name.

Side 2: For you are great and do wondrous things;

you alone are God. Teach me your way, O Lord, that I may walk in your truth; give me an undivided heart to revere your name.

Side 1: I give thanks to you, O Lord my God, with my whole heart, and I will glorify your name forever.
Side 2: For great is your steadfast love toward me; you have delivered my soul from the depths of Sheol.

Side 1: O God, the insolent rise up against me; a band of ruffians seeks my life, and they do not set you before them.
Side 2: But you, O Lord, are a God merciful and gracious, slow to anger and abounding in steadfast love and faithfulness.

Side 1: Turn to me and be gracious to me; give your strength to your servant; save the child of your serving girl.
Side 2: Show me a sign of your favor, so that those who hate me may see it and be put to shame, because you, Lord, have helped me and comforted me.

Closing Song: "The Lord Is My Light" by Christopher Walker (OCP)

A Prayer for Social Outreach Volunteers

Suggestion for use: *Begin a meeting of the social justice committee or any other group of social outreach volunteers by using this prayer to focus their concerns on the people they want to serve.*

Opening Song: "Find Us Ready" by Tom Booth (OCP)

Leader: Let us spend a few moments in silence, thinking about the people we want to serve. Imagine their situations and their needs. Find in yourself the gifts you want to offer.

Observe a short period of silence

Reader: Matthew 11:28–30

Response: Pray Psalm 23 slowly together.

Reader:

So many people are in such pain today. So many people are suffering and are in need of our understanding and support. But the questions remain: How can we do this in today's stressful world? What would a caring attitude involve for a person who wishes to embrace a full spiritual life?

Caring is "not in saying a lot of words to people, not in completing a compulsive list of works, and not in trying to respond to everyone's expectations (including our own!), but in trying, with all of our being, to develop an attitude of openness and alertness in our interactions with others which is based on only one thing: the desire to look for and bring God *everywhere*." And a cornerstone of such a wonderful form of caring is the beautiful gift of *presence*.[5]

Observe a few moments of silence.

Leader: Turn to someone near you, and in groups of two or three, take a few moments to talk about how the gift of presence is a form of caring. What would a caring attitude involve?

Allow time for sharing. Invite spontaneous prayer from the group: for people in need and for spiritual gifts for those present.

Closing Prayer: Psalm 27

Side 1: The Lord is my light and my salvation; whom shall I fear? The Lord is the stronghold of my life; of whom shall I be afraid?
Side 2: When evildoers assail me to devour my flesh—my adversaries and foes—they shall stumble and fall.

Side 1: Though an army encamp against me, my heart shall not fear; though war rise up against me, yet I will be confident.

Side 2: One thing I asked of the Lord, that will I seek after: to live in the house of the Lord all the days of my life, to behold the beauty of the Lord, and to inquire in his temple.

Side 1: For he will hide me in his shelter in the day of trouble; he will conceal me under the cover of his tent; he will set me high on a rock.

Side 2: Now my head is lifted up above my enemies all around me, and I will offer in his tent sacrifices with shouts of joy; I will sing and make melody to the Lord.

Side 1: Hear, O Lord, when I cry aloud, be gracious to me and answer me! "Come," my heart says, "seek his face!" Your face, Lord, do I seek.

Side 2: Do not hide your face from me. Do not turn your servant away in anger, you who have been my help. Do not cast me off, do not forsake me, O God of my salvation!

Side 1: If my father and mother forsake me, the Lord will take me up. Teach me your way, O Lord, and lead me on a level path because of my enemies.

Side 2: Do not give me up to the will of my adversaries, for false witnesses have risen against me, and they are breathing out violence.

Side 1: I believe that I shall see the goodness of the Lord in the land of the living.

Side 2: Wait for the Lord; be strong, and let your heart take courage; wait for the Lord!

Closing Song: "Eye Has Not Seen" by Marty Haugen (GIA)

A Prayer for Youth Groups

Suggestions for use: *This prayer could be used as part of a retreat day for teenagers, as an opening prayer before any gathering of the youth group or as a closing prayer to end a social or service activity. Have Scripture passages ready to hand out. (See the activity directions below regarding the reading from Hebrews.)*

Opening Song: "Here I Am" by Tom Booth (OCP)

Leader: God has promised to be with us, right beside us, through all dangers and struggles, in times of temptation and sadness, in all our rejoicing and achievements. God has said, "Here I am," and only asks us to believe this.

Reader: James 1:2–8

Youth Leader: That we may grow to see beyond ourselves,
All: We seek your help, O Lord.

Youth Leader: That we may live to know a world at peace,
All: We seek your help, O Lord.

Youth Leader: That we may rise above all petty strife,
All: We seek your help, O Lord.

Youth Leader: That we may know to call upon your name,
All: We seek your help, O Lord.

Youth Leader: That we may trust your friendship never ends,
All: We seek your help, O Lord.

Youth Leader: That we may give when called upon by you,
All: We seek your help, O Lord.

Youth Leader: God, our Father, Creator of all that is good and beautiful,
All: Help us become all that we can become.

Youth Leader: Jesus, our Brother, Savior of all that need redeeming,

All: Help us grow beyond our mistakes.

Youth Leader: Holy Spirit, our Counselor, Sanctifier of all who seek the way of truth,
All: Help us to walk the path of goodness.

Reader: Hebrews 13:1–3, 7–9, 14–17, 20–21

Activity: Divide the participants into at least four groups. Give each group a segment of the reading from Hebrews, which they have just heard: 13:1–3; 13:7–9; 13:14–17; 13:20–21. Instruct them to read it slowly, to take a quiet moment to think about the words, and to share with each other a couple words or a phrase that was particularly meaningful. After allowing time for this, bring the whole group together and invite general comments on this experience. Was anyone moved to some new awareness? Would anyone consider praying this way when using a Bible for private prayer or with a small group of friends?

Read the entire passage again to the whole group.

Youth Leader: For the many times and ways we succeed.
All: Praise and bless the Lord!

Youth Leader: For the courage to try again after failures.
All: Praise and bless the Lord!

Youth Leader: For all the love that comes to us from many people.
All: Praise and bless the Lord!

Youth Leader: For the healing that comes when we feel unloved.
All: Praise and bless the Lord!

Youth Leader: For the answers we discover when we question life.
All: Praise and bless the Lord!

Youth Leader: For the questions we encounter when we dare to live.
All: Praise and bless the Lord!

Youth Leader: God, Our Father, Wisdom of the ages.
All: We thank you for all you have revealed to us.

Youth Leader: Jesus, our Brother, Teacher and Healer.
All: We thank you for knowing us so well.

Youth Leader: Holy Spirit, our Counselor, bringer of Light.
All: We thank you for every inspiration.

Youth Leader: With the Father, Son and Holy Spirit, we offer to the world the gift of our youth and enthusiasm, our God-given talents, our idealism and abilities. Bearing your blessing and hearing your call, our Trinity God, we find the confidence to bring hope to our world. Help us touch our innate goodness so we can shine forth as sparks of your love.
All: Amen.

Closing Song: "I Am the Light of the World" by Greg Hayakawa (OCP)

Ritual movement with lighted candles for each individual could be used with the closing song, especially in a retreat setting.

PART VI

☩

Prayer Services: Sacraments

Prayer for Preparing for Baptism

Suggestion for atmosphere: Display the symbolic items that will be used at the time of baptism: water, oil, candle, white garment or stole. This prayer can be used with parents who are preparing for the baptism of their children or with adults who are preparing for their own baptism.

Opening Song: "Gather Your People" (verses 2 and 4) by Bob Hurd (OCP)

Leader: We have come together to think about, and to pray about, what it means to be baptized into a community of faith in Jesus. As we prepare for baptism (or for the baptism of our children), let us be open to the ways God's Word can touch our hearts.

First Reading: Ephesians 1:3–10

Leader: What does it mean to be baptized? The symbols are powerful: flowing water speaks of life that is fresh and new, sparkling and moving, ready to quench the thirst for adventure and discovery as the baptized person embraces the journey of a life guided by faith; anointing with oil marks the recipient as a chosen one called by God to use gifts and talents for building a kingdom of love in which all will feel welcome and at home; the flame from the candle shows a light to the world proclaiming the reality of God's light in the soul; the white garment announces being clothed in the virtues to which Jesus called his followers: kindness, humility, sinlessness, love and forgiveness.

With these symbols to teach and remind us, we approach the sacrament of Baptism with reverence and awe. There is mystery here. God calls us as God's own. The Lord anoints us and the Spirit breathes in us.

Through faith, we are brought together into a community. It is a community that pledges to support us when life is difficult, to rekindle the flame when faith weakens, to wrap the cloak of kindness around us when we feel alone, to share our joy when the journey is pure delight. We are not asked to walk without companions. Baptism is a pledge to and from the community.

To be baptized is to have a home in a family of believers. To be baptized is to take up the challenge to live the Christian call to love and service. To be baptized is to be aware of God's love.

Let us pause to reflect.

All: We thank you, Lord, for calling us to this family of believers. We pledge to take up the challenge to live a life of love and service according to the teachings of Jesus. We will do our best to witness to your love through the way we treat others. By your grace, we will choose holiness as you have chosen us. Amen.

Second Reading: Romans 6:3–11

Response: Psalm 67

All: May God be gracious to us and bless us and make his face to shine upon us.

Psalm Leader: May your way be known upon earth, your saving power among all nations. Let the peoples praise you, O God; let all the peoples praise you.
All: May God be gracious to us and bless us and make his face to shine upon us.

Psalm Leader: Let the nations be glad and sing for joy, for you judge the peoples with equity and guide the nations upon earth. Let the peoples praise you, O God; let all the peoples praise you.
All: May God be gracious to us and bless us and make his face to shine upon us.

Psalm Leader: The earth has yielded its increase; God, our God, has blessed us. May God continue to bless us; let all the ends of the earth revere him.
All: May God be gracious to us and bless us and make his face to shine upon us.

Leader: All respond "Amen" to each part of the blessing.

Leader: May you die to sinful ways and rise to new life.
All: Amen.

Leader: May you walk blameless in God's sight.
All: Amen.

Leader: May the glory of God fill your mind and heart forever.
All: Amen

Closing Song: "Let the River Flow" by Darrel Evans (Mercy/ Vineyard)

Prayer for Preparing for Eucharist

Suggestion for use: This prayer and activity could be used during a class for parents and children when families are preparing a child for the experience of First Eucharist. Have drawing paper and markers available, as well as the Mass parts descriptions given below.

Opening Song: "Song of the Body of Christ" by David Haas (GIA)

Leader: We come to share our story and it is the story of Jesus—a life spent in love and given in sacrifice. We are here tolearn how to participate more fully in the Mass, which remembers Jesus. We are here to learn that we are the Body of Christ, and being that Body carries responsibilities and graces. Let us listen to what the Scriptures tell us about Jesus' gift to us in the Eucharist.

First Reader: 1 Corinthians 10:16–17

Response: Psalm 95:1–7

Psalm Leader: Come, let us sing to the Lord; let us make a joyful noise to the rock of our salvation!

All: Come, let us sing to the Lord.

Psalm Leader: Let us come into his presence with thanksgiving; let us make a joyful noise to him with songs of praise!
All: Come, let us sing to the Lord.

Psalm Leader: For the Lord is a great God, and a great king above all gods. In his hand are the depths of the earth; the heights of the mountains are his also.
All: Come, let us sing to the Lord.

Psalm Leader: The sea is his, for he made it, and the dry land, which his hands have formed.
All: Come, let us sing to the Lord.

Psalm Leader: Come, let us worship and bow down, let us kneel before the Lord, our Maker! For he is our God, and we are the people of his pasture, and the sheep of his hand. O that today you would listen to his voice!
All: Come, let us sing to the Lord.

Second Reader: John 6:51, 54–58

Leader: What we have just been doing here is like the part of every Mass called the "Liturgy of the Word." Some Scriptures are read and people respond. This is a very important part of the Mass. There are other important parts, too. Right now each family will receive a description of some part of the Mass. You will also receive drawing paper and markers. Discuss an appropriate symbol for that part of the Mass and draw it on the paper. When all are finished, you will share your ideas with the whole group.

Give a handout about the parts of the Mass (below) to each family. Depending on the size of the class, there may be several families for each part, but ask the families to work individually.

■ *Photocopy the next page on "Parts of the Mass" for the group.*

Parts of the Mass

INTRODUCTORY RITES

When people enter the church, they use holy water to sign themselves with the cross. It is a reminder of their baptism. The Mass begins with a procession and a song. Then the priest greets the people and leads them through a penitential rite to call on God's mercy for the times we have sinned.

What would be an appropriate symbol you could make to express what happens in this first part of the Mass?

LITURGY OF THE WORD

Scripture readings are proclaimed to the people and people respond with prayer or song. After the Gospel, everyone listens to a homily that explains the lessons given through the Scriptures. Then all profess their faith by saying the Creed. The community prays for the needs in the world using "intercessions."

What would be an appropriate symbol you could make to express what happens in this second part of the Mass?

OFFERING OF GIFTS

The Liturgy of the Eucharist is the part of the Mass that begins with an offering of gifts. Bread and wine are brought to the altar, representing an offering of ourselves so God can transform us. Money is also collected sometimes so people can offer a gift for the needs of the church and those the church serves.

What would be an appropriate symbol you could make to express what happens in this third part of the Mass?

EUCHARISTIC PRAYER

Eucharist is a Greek word that means "thanksgiving." The prayers the priest says as he blesses the bread and wine are prayers of thanks and praise to God. Words of consecration, used by Jesus at the Last Supper, change the bread and wine to the body and blood of Jesus. The people's great "Amen" at the conclusion of the Eucharistic prayer is an expression of faith. "Amen" means "I believe" or "so be it."

What would be an appropriate symbol you could make to express what happens in this fourth part of the Mass?

COMMUNION RITE

This part of the Mass begins with everyone praying the Our Father. Then we exchange a greeting of peace with those around us. It is important to be at peace with people before receiving Jesus. The "Lamb of God" prayer is spoken or sung. Then people receive Communion. Time for singing and time for quiet prayer are appropriate during the communion ritual.

What would be an appropriate symbol you could make to express what happens in this fifth part of the Mass?

DISMISSAL

At the end of Mass, the priest sends the people out to live the lessons they have learned from the Scriptures and to take to others the Jesus they have received in their hearts. They can do this by loving and serving people as Jesus would. A final song concludes the Mass as the priest leaves the altar area.

What would be an appropriate symbol you could make to express what happens in this sixth part of the Mass?

When families are finished, assemble the whole group and, starting with part one, ask one or more members of every family who had that part to come forward with their drawing. From several families, there may be a variety of symbols. Invite a spokesperson from each family to explain their symbol. Do this with each Mass part.

Leader: During the Liturgy of the Eucharist, shortly before you receive Communion, you will hear the priest say words like these over the bread and wine. This is from the Gospel of Mark:

Reader: Mark 14:22–25

Leader: Let us pray to Jesus, who gives us this gift of Eucharist.
All: Jesus, prepare our minds to understand your gift. Prepare our hearts to receive you in love and with gratitude. Prepare our wills to choose to serve others as you did. Help us to be worthy members of your Body, the church. Amen.

Song: "Seed, Scattered and Sown" by Dan Feiten (Ekklesia)

Prayer for Preparing for Reconciliation

Suggestion for use: This is a prayer service to use with parents and children when families are preparing their children for a first experience with the sacrament of reconciliation. The prayer can be used during a preparation class, particularly at the end of the class. Have a second room ready for the time when parents and children are split up for their examination of conscience (see below).

Opening Song: "Remember Your Love" (verses 1, 2 and 3) by Darryl Ducote, Gary Daigle (Damean Music)

All: We come to you God, trusting in your love and forgiveness. We know that through our lifetime we will often have need of your mercy. Help us now to prepare ourselves and our families for an encounter with you soon in the sacrament of forgiveness.

First Reader: 1 John 5:1–5

Response: Psalm 128

Psalm Leader: Happy is everyone who fears the Lord, who walks in his ways. You shall eat the fruit of the labor of your hands; you shall be happy, and it shall go well with you.
All: Help us to obey your commandments, O God.

Psalm Leader: Your wife will be like a fruitful vine within your house; your children will be like olive shoots around your table. Thus shall the man be blessed who fears the Lord.
All: Help us to obey your commandments, O God.

Psalm Leader: The Lord bless you from Zion. May you see the prosperity of Jerusalem all the days of your life. May you see your children's children. Peace be upon Israel!
All: Help us to obey your commandments, O God.

Second Reader: Luke 15:3–7

Leader: We have heard and we believe that God seeks what is lost. God takes care of those who lose their way and is happy to bring them home again. Sometimes we aren't even aware of how we have lost our way, so it is good to take time to think about our actions. As practice for the way we will be preparing to confess our failings in the sacrament of reconciliation, we will take a little time now to examine our lives in terms of our relationships, our responsibilities and our connection with God. The questions for an examination of conscience will be different for parents and children, so one teacher will take the children to another room for this part.

A teacher takes the children to a separate room. The leader for each group then conducts the examination of conscience, using the appropriate set of questions, below. Designate a time for the children to return.

Examination of Conscience for Parents

Use this examination of conscience with the parents, pausing after each question.

Leader: Let us examine our relationships: Is there anyone I have not forgiven? Do I seek to understand people with a different viewpoint? Have I expressed my love to family and friends? Do I gossip or damage reputations? Am I sensitive to others' feelings? Do I make time for relationships?

Let us examine our responsibilities: Do I contribute time and resources when others need me? Do I earn my living honestly? Am I a good neighbor? Do I care for whatever has been entrusted to me? Do I take responsibility for forming and following a good conscience? Have I shirked my duties or put blame on others for my shortcomings?

Let us examine our response to God: Do I pray daily? Am I interested in my spiritual development? Do I allow God to direct my life? Have I taken an active role in my church community? Do I have Jesus' love for the poor, the outcasts, the sinners? Do I value and take part in the sacramental life of the church?

Examination of Conscience for Children

Use this examination of conscience with the children, pausing after each question. The teacher could lead a very brief discussion, sharing ideas and examples, after each of the three parts of the examination.

Teacher: Let us think about our family and friends: Do I respect and obey my parents? Am I kind to my brothers and sisters? Do I share with family members and friends? Am I nice to my friends even when I don't want something from them? Am I willing to be a friend to someone who needs one?

Optional: Allow time for discussion.

Let us think about our work and play: Do I do chores at home without complaining? Do I do school work willingly so I can grow and learn? Do I play fair, take turns and work well on teams? Am I a peacemaker, staying away from violence in video games, movies and sports? Do I make peace with friends? Am I gentle to God's creatures and responsible about taking care of pets?

Optional: Allow time for discussion.

Let us think about our God and church: Do I talk to God every day? Do I believe Jesus is with me wherever I am? Am I interested in learning what God teaches me through the Bible? Do I come to church, behave in church and make friends with my parish family? Do I love God with all my heart?

Optional: Allow time for discussion.

When the families are together again, conclude with one more Scripture reading.

First Reader: 1 Peter 3:8–12

All: Thank you, God, for this preparation time. Thank you for the reminders of how we can love you and others better. Bless us when we leave here and help us to remember what we have prayed about today. Help us to turn away from evil and to seek peace. Amen.

Closing Song: "Through It All" by Andrae Crouch/Peter Quint (Manna Music, Inc.)

Prayer for Preparing for Confirmation

Suggestion for use: Use this prayer in the context of a confirmation class for teenagers or young adults. It could also be used when studying confirmation with an RCIA group.

Opening Song: "Send Us Your Spirit" by David Haas (GIA)

Reader: Sirach 24:1–9, 16–17

Response: Sirach 24:19–22, 32–33

Side 1: Come to me, you who desire Wisdom, and eat your fill of my fruits.

Side 2: For the memory of me is sweeter than honey, and the possession of me sweeter than the honeycomb.

Side 1: Those who eat of me will hunger for more, and those who drink of me will thirst for more.

Side 2: Whoever obeys me will not be put to shame, and those who work with me will not sin.

Side 1: I will again make instruction shine forth like the dawn, and I will make it clear from far away.

Side 2: I will again pour out teaching like prophecy, and leave it to all future generations.

Reader: Luke 1:26–33

Reflection: The first reading, from the book of Sirach, shows us Wisdom singing her own praises. That's a delightful image! She declares her own worth in the presence of the Most High. What heartwarming audacity! And what gives her the confidence to do this? "I came forth from the mouth of the Most High," she says. Her origin is divine. She was conceived by God—and emerged from God—and is the beloved of God. Her confidence is well placed.

And so she spreads out her branches, "glorious and graceful," and God's covenant with the people of the earth overflows with wisdom. That we might help to build the reign of God together, let us adopt the confidence and audacity of Wisdom. Let us acknowledge that we were conceived by God and born of God's plan. Let us recognize that we have always been and continue to be loved by God. Let us not be afraid to spread out branches. Let Wisdom be our guide.

In the Gospel of Luke, a humble Mary, fearful of an angel's message, is told that she will conceive and bear the Son of God. Mary's littleness is a counterbalance to Wisdom's show of confidence. The humility *and* the trust, the fear of the unknown *and* the joy of being loved, the human *and* the divine—these all work hand in hand to make possible a kingdom of God whose reign will have no end. What a lesson there is in that for us!

We cannot know what exactly will transpire in our livesover the years. But, as we prepare for our confirmation during the days ahead, we can take with us the lessons this Gospel teaches us.

The Gospel is about:
- the humility of Mary who didn't know if she could do the job she was being asked to do.
- the infusion of the Spirit into a common, ordinary life to produce extraordinary results.
- not knowing the future, but putting everything in God's hands with perfect trust.
- being faithful in little things, grateful for simple things, joyful about all things.

We often expect great things from life:
- We want to be able to handle all problems, tackle all the big tasks, understand everything.
- We want great vision to know where we are going and how we are going to get there.
- We want great results and tangible evidence that something worthwhile happened.
- We want great religious experiences that will move us, inspire us, speak to us, bond us.
- We want special ways and great fun to socialize, to laugh, to share, to be together.

• We have great expectations of being loved and of tasting success.

But the Gospel we heard today is about littleness! Now this doesn't mean we shouldn't have any great expectations. But let's put those great expectations in our God.

Let us expect:
• that the Holy Spirit, in wisdom, will inspire us.
• that Jesus, in goodness, will teach and heal us.
• that God, with power and love, will create a future we can only begin to imagine.

And, while having these great expectations of our God, let us keep littleness for ourselves. Let us have the humility to receive guidance from the Spirit—in our prayer lives, in our relationships, in our faith and vision. Let us have the humility to learn from Jesus about service, about believing in miracles, about laying down our lives. Let us have the humility to be molded and used by our God for whatever the future is for the church and for the needs of the world.

Let us prepare for confirmation with the spirit of Wisdom and with the spirit of Mary. Let us ask the Holy Spirit to come to us and to help us.

Follow this reflection with the meditation song: "Ruah" by Liam Lawton from the album In the Quiet *(GIA)*

Leader: The Hebrew name for the Spirit of God is *Ruah*, the breath of God that hovers over creation and brings it to life. We are preparing for and praying for the Spirit of God to come to us and bring us to fullness of life. Respond to each intercession with: "Ruah, Spirit of God, fill us with your life."

Leader: That we may be inspired to live a life of service
All: "Ruah, Spirit of God, fill us with your life."

Leader: That we may receive wisdom and strength for life's journey
All: "Ruah, Spirit of God, fill us with your life."

Leader: That we may be healed of doubts and fears and may learn to bring this healing to others also
All: "Ruah, Spirit of God, fill us with your life."

Leader: That we may be touched by the wonder and beauty of our God
All: "Ruah, Spirit of God, fill us with your life."

Leader: That we may be enlightened and guided by Truth
All: "Ruah, Spirit of God, fill us with your life."

Leader: That we may grow in compassion and selflessness
All: "Ruah, Spirit of God, fill us with your life."

Leader: Let us pray. With the humility of Mary and the audacity of Wisdom, we name ourselves your servants and your offspring. With great joy, God, we delight in your love for us. With hope we await the manifestations of your Spirit touching our lives. We continue to walk with Jesus, who teaches in your name. Amen.

Closing Song: "Sometimes by Step" by Rich Mullins and Beaker (BMG)

Prayer for Preparing for Marriage

Suggestion for uses: *This is a prayer service for engaged couples who are preparing for marriage. It could be used to begin or to conclude a marriage preparation class.*

Opening Song: "We Are One Body" by Dana Scallon (Heartbeat Music/August Music)

Leader: At the beginning of a life together, there is a strong desire that the union will truly be blessed, that all will work out well, that the inevitable trials and losses will be bearable and that love will overcome every obstacle. Saint Paul, in his letter to the Romans, describes the characteristics of a true Christian. His words could also apply to the characteristics of a true marriage.

Reader: Romans 12:9–12

Leader: As a response to these exhortations, let us pray this litany of intercessions:

Men: God, you created the love that is in our hearts.

Women: Help us to nurture it and keep our love alive forever.

Men: God, you call us to create a family.

Women: Bless all who will share our home and our lives.

Men: God, you have given us a community of family and friends.

Women: Give us the humility and wisdom to rely on their support.

All: Lord, you have been our dwelling place in all generations.

Women: Jesus, your life of love and sacrifice inspires us.

Men: Strengthen us to love well when sacrifices are hard to make.

Women: Jesus, you gathered disciples to make them followers of God's way.

Men: Teach us that way and make our lives an example to others.

Women: Jesus, you called little children to come to you.

Men: Make us receptive to the children who come into our lives.

All: Lord, you have been our dwelling place in all generations.

Men: Spirit of God, you fill us with a passion for loving.

Women: May the fire of your love spread through us to all we meet.

Men: Spirit of God, you open minds and speak to hearts.

Women: Touch us with your gifts of understanding and tolerance.

Men: Spirit of God, you fill your faithful ones with gentle confidence.

Women: Be with us as we commit our lives to each other and to you forever.

All: Lord, you have been our dwelling place in all generations. (Psalm 90:1)

Reader: 1 Peter 4:8–11

Leader: In anticipation of your wedding day, I ask you now to hold your partner's hand and bow your heads as we allow this blessing song to flow over us.

Closing Song: "When This Day Is Done" by Liam Lawton from the album In the Quiet, GIA

Alternate Closing Song: Hold hands, but all sing… "Wherever You Go" by Weston Priory: Gregory Norbert, o.s.b., Benedictine Foundation

Prayer for Preparing for Ordination

Suggestion for use: Use this prayer during a retreat with seminarians or deacons or as an opening prayer before a class.

Opening Song: "Here I Am, Lord" by Dan Schutte (OCP)

Leader: You are preparing to become ministers in service to God's Word and bearing God's compassionate love. Listen to the prayer of

Solomon for wisdom, and pray that you also may be wise.

Reader: Wisdom 9:1–4, 8–11

Response: Wisdom 10

Side 1: Wisdom protected the first-formed father of the world, when he alone had been created; she delivered him from his transgression and gave him strength to rule all things.

Side 2: But when an unrighteous man departed from her in his anger, he perished because in rage he killed his brother.

Side 1: When the earth was flooded because of him, wisdom again saved it, steering the righteous man by a paltry piece of wood.

Side 2: Wisdom also, when the nations in wicked agreement had been put to confusion, recognized the righteous man and preserved him blameless before God and kept him strong in the face of his compassion for his child.

Side 1: Wisdom rescued a righteous man when the ungodly were perishing; he escaped the fire that descended on the five cities.

Side 2: Evidence of their wickedness still remains: a continually smoking wasteland, plants bearing fruit that does not ripen and a pillar of salt standing as a monument to an unbelieving soul.

Side 1: For because they passed wisdom by, they not only were hindered from recognizing the good, but also left for humankind a reminder of their folly, so that their failures could never go unnoticed.

Side 2: Wisdom rescued from troubles those who served her. When a righteous man fled from his brother's wrath, she guided him on straight paths; she showed him the kingdom of God and gave him knowledge of holy things; she prospered him in his labors and increased the fruit of his toil.

Side 1: When his oppressors were covetous, she stood by him and made him rich. She protected him from his enemies and kept him safe from those who lay in wait for him; in his arduous contest she gave him the victory; so that he might learn that godliness is more powerful than anything else.

Side 2: When a righteous man was sold, wisdom did not desert him but delivered him from sin. She descended with him into the dungeon, and when he was in prison she did not leave him, until she brought him the scepter of a kingdom and authority over his masters. Those who accused him she showed to be false; and she gave him everlasting honor.

Side 1: A holy people and blameless race wisdom delivered from a nation of oppressors. She entered the soul of a servant of the Lord and withstood dread kings with wonders and signs.

Side 2: She gave to holy people the reward of their labors; she guided them along a marvelous way and became a shelter to them by day, and a starry flame through the night.

Side 1: She brought them over the Red Sea and led them through deep waters; but she drowned their enemies and cast them up from the depth of the sea.

Side 2: Therefore, the righteous plundered the ungodly; they sang hymns, O Lord, to your holy name and praised with one accord your defending hand; for wisdom opened the mouths of those who were mute and made the tongues of infants speak clearly.

Reader: Luke 10:1–11

REFLECTION

Commitments have personal purposes as well as social ones. In order to learn what life is meant to teach us, we must keep ourselves from running away from life when it gets hard, when it finally begins to demand something from us, when it asks far more from us than we ever expected to be able to give. Fidelity is not standing in place for the sake of being able to say we stood there. Fidelity is the potter's kiln of life where, tried by heat and flame, we change into shapes and glazes of which we never dreamed.... What we must be faithful to is the beckoning God, who goes before us into human history healing what is wounded, raising up what is good in us for all to see and calling us to do the same.[6]

Response: Beckoning God, keep us faithful to you.

Leader: When commitments are challenging and people are ungrateful...
All: Beckoning God, keep us faithful to you.

Leader: When we are tried by fire and tempted to resist how you are shaping us.
All: Beckoning God, keep us faithful to you.

Leader: When we do not see the goodness you have placed in us.
All: Beckoning God, keep us faithful to you.

Leader: When we feel the pain of a world that is wounded.
All: Beckoning God, keep us faithful to you.

Leader: When we see, through your eyes, the gifts that we could call forth from others.
All: Beckoning God, keep us faithful to you.

Leader: When we are proclaiming that the kingdom of God is near.
All: Beckoning God, keep us faithful to you.

Leader: Let us pray. When you commission us, Lord, as you commissioned your disciples, give us Wisdom as our companion and your example as our guide. Ordain us for service and keep us humbly aware that our call is to holiness. May we be pleasing in your sight all the days of our lives. Amen.

Closing Song: "The Summons" by John L. Bell (GIA)

Prayer for Preparing for Anointing of the Sick

Suggestions for atmosphere: The Scriptures, music and guided imagery in this prayer service can lead right into the anointing of a group who has gathered to receive this sacrament. Be sure to provide comfortable seating and maintain a quiet, peaceful setting. If available, a fountain with flowing water could be turned on during the guided imagery.

Leader: We have come together to seek healing, and so we will begin by turning to the Scriptures for comfort.

First Reader: Philippians 4:4–7

Response: Psalm 42

Side 1: As a deer longs for flowing streams, so my soul longs for you, O God. My soul thirsts for God, for the living God. When shall I come and behold the face of God?
Side 2: My tears have been my food day and night, while people say to me continually, "Where is your God?"

Side 1: These things I remember, as I pour out my soul: how I went with the throng and led them in procession to the house of God, with glad shouts and songs of thanksgiving, a multitude keeping festival.
Side 2: Why are you cast down, O my soul, and why are you disquieted within me? Hope in God; for I shall again praise him, my help and my God.

Side 1: My soul is cast down within me; therefore, I remember you from the land of Jordan and of Hermon, from Mount Mizar.
Side 2: Deep calls to deep at the thunder of your cataracts; all your waves and your billows have gone over me.

Side 1: By day the Lord commands his steadfast love, and at night his song is with me, a prayer to the God of my life.

Side 2: I say to God, my rock, "Why have you forgotten me? Why must I walk about mournfully because the enemy oppresses me?"

Side 1: As with a deadly wound in my body, my adversaries taunt me, while they say to me continually, "Where is your God?"

Side 2: Why are you cast down, O my soul, and why are you disquieted within me? Hope in God, for I shall again praise him, my help and my God.

Second Reader: John 7:37–38

Song: "You Are Mine" by David Haas (GIA)

This song is preparation for the guided imagery experience which follows. It can be used to sing along with, or as a listening meditation.

GUIDED MEDITATION

Leader: Close your eyes, slow down and deepen your breathing. Relax the muscles in your head, neck, shoulders, limbs. Let go of intruding thoughts, current concerns. Simply be in the present moment and enter into visualizing the images to which you will be guided.

If there is a fountain, turn it on at this time. Quiet instrumental music could also be played. Pause after each phrase, with a longer pause after each paragraph.

Imagine yourself in an outdoor place of deep peace. There is soft music in the background. You can hear water flowing, though you cannot see the source of that sound. Birds are chirping, and occasionally you see them hop or fly by. The air is comfortably warm and you can feel every part of you relaxing. The worry, pain, anxiety and discomfort are all slipping away. Focus only on the music, the sound of water, the birds, the air.

Into the stillness comes a comforting Presence. Though you can't see anyone, you know the Presence is the spirit of Jesus. Jesus comes to you as Healer. He assures you that he understands your needs and cares about your concerns. He reminds you of God's love and tells you that love will touch you in many ways through many people if you are open to receive it. Hear these reassurances and feel the truth in these promises.

Jesus says, "Come to me, you who thirst. I am living water and will refresh you." Now you know the source of the water you were hearing. It is the Healer. Every time you hear water in the future, you will remember that Jesus wants to heal you.

Imagine yourself free from all worry and pain. Imagine exactly how you wish to feel and how you want to live. Let that image become real. Choose the path of healing; embrace liberation from sickness. Watch Jesus become visible to you now, smiling, nodding, encouraging: "If you want, I can make you whole. Be healed."

The sound of water fades, but you know it will come again often. The deep peace continues. You feel totally refreshed and ready to handle the burdens and joys of living. Soon you will be anointed for the task of moving toward healing. When you feel ready for this, open your eyes.

The celebrant can now proceed with the ritual for the sacrament of anointing of the sick.

Closing Song: "There Is a Well" ("*Un Pozo Hay*") by Tom Conry (OCP)

PART VII

✢

Prayer Services for Special Concerns

Prayer During Times of Division

Suggestion for use: Sometimes issues and disagreements divide people in a community. Progress can't be made and healing can't happen until the unity is restored. This prayer can be used while the division still exists. Its purpose is to invite the participants to be open to seeing all sides and to remind them of the love and common purpose that exist in the community.

Opening Song: "One Spirit, One Church" by Kevin Keil (OCP)

Leader: This is not a time for making decisions; nor is it a time for discussion. Our community is divided, though we profess unity in the Spirit of God. As with any family, this family of believers has its disagreements. At no time, however, do we forget that we sincerely love one another in Christ. We call on the Holy Spirit, the Comforter, to bring grace and heavenly aid to our troubled hearts.

We will listen to God's Word, reminding us of our noble calling. We will spend time in silent prayer, opening to the Spirit's presence. We will pray to end our division. This is a courageous prayer. We come before God, together, with faith and trust.

First Reader: Ephesians 4:29—5:2

Observe an extended period of silence.

Leader: That we may receive people with understanding,
All: Open our minds and hearts, O Lord.

Leader: That we may not be quick to judge,
All: Open our minds and hearts, O Lord.

Leader: That we may grow in tolerance and acceptance,
All: Open our minds and hearts, O Lord.

Leader: When we are tempted to impose our ideas on others,
All: Open our minds and hearts, O Lord.

Leader: When we are tempted to ridicule or belittle someone else's opinion,
All: Open our minds and hearts, O Lord.

Leader: When we are tempted to be smug or superior,
All: Open our minds and hearts, O Lord.

Second Reader: James 3:13–18

Observe an extended period of silence.

Leader: Seeing the goodness in so many people who live by faith,
All: We rejoice in your greatness, O God.

Leader: Seeing the efforts of so many who want to do what is right,
All: We rejoice in your greatness, O God.

Leader: Seeing the gifts and abilities of those who want to serve,
All: We rejoice in your greatness, O God.

Leader: Believing that the Spirit is moving among us in many ways,
All: We rejoice in your greatness, O God.

Leader: Believing that people were created in the image of goodness,
All: We rejoice in your greatness, O God.

Leader: Believing that ultimately everything is being drawn to union with you,
All: We rejoice in your greatness, O God.

Leader: Let us offer to one another a sign of peace.

Leader: Let us pray.
All: It is with profound humility and awe that we bow before you, God, setting aside our differences and bitter feuds. We acknowledge our guilt in perpetuating division. We call on you to collapse our walls and dissolve our boundaries so we may move toward healing and forgiveness. May we see all people as chosen people and no one as unloved by you. We ask this in the name of all that is good and holy when you are in our midst. Amen.

Closing Song: "Great Is the Power We Proclaim" by Christopher Walker (OCP)

Prayer Before Making a Decision

Suggestion for use: *Any parish group can use this prayer when it is preparing to make an important decision about something. The focus here is on how Jesus turned to prayer before making major decisions in his life.*

Opening Song: "Go Light Your World" by Chris Rice (BMG)

Leader: Before making the important decision(s) we have to make, let us seek wisdom. Wisdom is personified in the Old Testament as an image of God. Solomon valued her and won God's favor by preferring her more than riches.

Reader: Wisdom 6:12–16; 7:24–28

Response: Psalm 85:1–2, 7–13

Leader: Lord, you were favorable to your land; you restored the fortunes of Jacob. You forgave the iniquity of your people; you pardoned all their sin.
All: Lead us to wisdom, Lord.

Leader: Show us your steadfast love, O Lord, and grant us your salvation. Let me hear what God the Lord will speak, for he will speak peace to his people, to his faithful, to those who turn to him in their hearts.
All: Lead us to wisdom, Lord.

Leader: Surely his salvation is at hand for those who fear him, that his glory may dwell in our land. Steadfast love and faithfulness will meet; righteousness and peace will kiss each other.
All: Lead us to wisdom, Lord

Leader: Faithfulness will spring up from the ground, and righteousness will look down from the sky.
All: Lead us to wisdom, Lord

Leader: The Lord will give what is good, and our land will yield its increase. Righteousness will go before him, and will make a path for his steps.
All: Lead us to wisdom, Lord.

Leader: The Gospel of Luke particularly shows us that whenever Jesus was about to make a major decision, he took time to pray. The place he gave in his life to quiet time with God gives us an example to do the same.

Reader: Luke 3:21–22

Leader: Jesus' baptism was a prelude to his public ministry. In this scene we find him praying and receiving the Holy Spirit. Right after this the Spirit would lead him into the desert for a more extended period of prayer and fasting. It was essential to Jesus that he clarify what his public ministry should be, and he relied on prayer to help him do that.
All: Lord, we are seeking to be clear about our mission. We know that temptations could steer us away from our goals. Having been baptized by you and called to serve our community, we seek the Spirit's guidance. Bless us with insight.

Reader: Luke 6:12–13

Leader: When Jesus was going to choose the people who would be his closest companions, who would learn from him and carry on his work, he did not make that decision without prayerful discernment. He spent the whole night communicating with God.
All: Lord, we have some choices to make. We know that the people who share in the results of our decisions are companions in our venture. Having seen the need to choose our direction wisely, we seek God's assistance. Bless us with answers.

Reader: Luke 11:1–4

Leader: Jesus' disciples understood that there was probably a right way to pray and a wrong way to pray. They had seen how Jesus resorted to prayer frequently, and they wanted to pray as he did.

All: Lord, we want our prayer to be about God's will. We know that your kingdom, your reign of love, must be our ultimate goal. Having been reminded to forgive and having been taught to expect that you will provide for all our needs, we seek to grow in trust. Bless us with patience.

Reader: Luke 21:36–38

Leader: As tension mounted during Jesus' ministry, he continued to advocate prayer and engage in prayer. This is how he found the strength to continue to face his adversaries.

All: Lord, we need the strength that comes from prayer. We know we may face opposition to our plans and decisions. Having been fortified by prayer that is honest and not self-serving, we seek to grow in confidence. Bless us with endurance.

Reader: Luke 22:39–46

Leader: To the end, Jesus persevered in prayer. To the end, he encouraged his disciples to join him in this. He saw prayer as very necessary preparation for life's hardships.

All: Lord, we expect some difficulties in the future. We know that decisions must always be evaluated and circumstances are always changing. Having determined to move ahead with making decisions, we seek your reliable support. Bless us with attentiveness.

Leader: Relying on prayer, as Jesus always did, we remember that God guides all our movements. With the insight, answers, patience, endurance and attentiveness we have requested as blessings from our God, let us take action with confidence.

Closing Song: "Go Make a Difference" by Steve Angrisano and Tom Tomaszek (OCP)

Prayer in Times of Transition

Suggestion for atmosphere: Arrange the seating in groups of three or four. Have papers prepared containing the questions used in the guided reflection (see the ten questions below). Don't distribute the papers until after the reflection. On a table in the front of the gathering place have a Bible, a poster showing the number 40 in large type, and pictures of Noah, Moses, Jesus and the apostles. Also provide the responses the participants will pray after each Scripture reading.

Opening Song: "Change Our Hearts" by Rory Cooney (OCP)

Leader: Change is never easy, even when it is a change we want. But life is all about change. Nothing remains the same. There is mystery in this. There is a dying or letting go that has to happen so something new can come to life.

I invite you to close your eyes and use a few quiet minutes to recall personal examples of letting go and experiencing change. What was difficult about it? What was exciting? What was the result? (*Pause for quiet reflection for about three minutes.*)

Turn to those around you in small groups of three or four and share your stories. (*Allow six to eight minutes for this.*)

Now return to the quiet within yourself. Again close your eyes. Recall your personal experiences of change and the feelings you had about them. Recall what was just shared with you by members of your group. How were their experiences and feelings similar to yours? How were they different?

Think now about the change we have come here to pray about today:

Pause after each question.

Why is this change happening (or why is it necessary)?

What will be difficult about it?

What new possibilities could open up?

How ready are we to embrace change?

How can we help others to deal with this change?

List all the positive outcomes your imagination can conceive.

What will be lost that the community needs to grieve?

Can we provide a way for them to grieve and celebrate what is passing?

Envision the future after the change takes place. Does this vision inspire hope?

How can that hope be conveyed to the community?

Open your eyes. You will now receive a piece of paper containing the questions you have just been thinking about. Discuss them with the same group with whom you shared your personal experiences. (*Allow twelve to fifteen minutes for this or longer, if this prayer is used in connection with a parish planning meeting regarding the change.*)

Now let us bring our reflection and discussion to prayer.

Leader: In Scripture the number forty is a symbol for transition time. Whenever a story is told in terms of forty years or forty days, for example, the number isn't literal. It is saying that the particular event is indicative of a significant change for the people involved. After hearing each Scripture story, we will respond with a prayer.

First Reader: Genesis 7:17–23; 8:6–7
All: As Noah experienced the loss of a world in transition and then found that life could renew itself, so also do we ride the waves of change. Help us, Lord, to let go of whatever is no longer life-giving. Lead us to the new life we will help create.

Second Reader: Exodus 34:27–32
All: As Moses experienced a life-changing direction while he communed with God on Mt. Sinai, so also do we seek direction and guid-

ance for the changes we are facing. Help us, Lord, to know your will for us. Inspire us with a plan of action.

Third Reader: Exodus 16:35
All: As the Israelites needed time to become a community and to grow in their knowledge of the God of the Covenant, so also do we need a period of time to grow into our new commitments. Help us, Lord, to use our transition time for bonding as a community. Nourish us with your presence on our journey.

Fourth Reader: Matthew 4:1–11
All: As Jesus transitioned into a public life by taking time for prayer and for struggling with how to shape his ministry, so also do we need to be attentive to our inner conflicts. Help us, Lord, to take time for prayer and to come to peace with our turmoil. Strengthen us with your vision.

Fifth Reader: Acts 1:1–5
All: As the apostles needed time to understand how the resurrected Jesus was with them in a new way, so also do we need time, during this period of change, to find God in what is becoming. Help us, Lord, to recognize you in the many ways you come to us. Give us your Holy Spirit to guide us through our time of transition. Amen.

Closing Song: "City of God" by Dan Schutte (OCP)

Prayer Before a Finance Meeting

Suggestion for atmosphere: Display on a prayer table symbols of parish resources, finances, physical accomplishments, donations (examples: budget, photos of new or remodeled facilities or acquisitions, announcements of donations or pictures of organizations or people who received financial assistance from the parish).

Opening Song: "Lead Me, Lord" by John D. Becker (OCP)

Leader: Knowing we are blessed in our giving and knowing that our finance committee exists in order to serve, we offer our prayer today asking God to make us good stewards of our resources. In both the Old Testament and the New Testament communities, the people of God were instructed to share what they possessed. Let us listen to some examples and take these instructions to heart.

First Reader: Tobit 4:7–11

Second Reader: Acts 4:32–35

Response: Psalm 33:1–15, 18–22

Side 1: Rejoice in the Lord, O you righteous. Praise befits the upright. Praise the Lord with the lyre; make melody to him with the harp of ten strings.

Side 2: Sing to him a new song; play skillfully on the strings, with loud shouts. For the word of the Lord is upright, and all his work is done in faithfulness. He loves righteousness and justice; the earth is full of the steadfast love of the Lord.

Side 1: By the word of the Lord the heavens were made, and all their host by the breath of his mouth. He gathered the waters of the sea as in a bottle; he put the deeps in storehouses.

Side 2: Let all the earth fear the Lord; let all the inhabitants of the world stand in awe of him. For he spoke, and it came to be; he commanded, and it stood firm.

Side 1: The Lord brings the counsel of the nations to nothing; he frustrates the plans of the peoples. The counsel of the Lord stands forever, the thoughts of his heart to all generations.

Side 2: Happy is the nation whose God is the Lord, the people whom he has chosen as his heritage. The Lord looks down from heaven; he sees all humankind.

Side 1: From where he sits enthroned he watches all the inhabitants of the earth—he who fashions the hearts of them all, and observes all their deeds.

Side 2: Truly the eye of the Lord is on those who fear him, on those who hope in his steadfast love, to deliver their soul from death, and to keep them alive in famine.

Side 1: Our soul waits for the Lord; he is our help and shield. Our heart is glad in him, because we trust in his holy name.

Side 2: Let your steadfast love, O Lord, be upon us, even as we hope in you.

Reading: Matthew 6:25–33

Leader: We have been given gifts by a loving God: the gift of life with all its opportunities to grow, the gift of earth with all her beauty and wonder, the gift of love with its power to transform, the gift of relationships with endless opportunities for meaningful interaction.

We are gifted with intellect and emotion and a drive to accomplish. We are gifted with sensitivity and wisdom and insight. Because of our God-given abilities, we are entrusted with many things.

As we reflect on the responsibilities of stewardship, let us keep always, before our minds and in our hearts, the remembrance that all is gift from a loving God.

If there are times when our resources seem to be less than sufficient, let us focus our trust on God who always provides just what we need. If there are times when blessed abundance has poured over us, let us be generous in sharing what we have. May our eyes be turned outward to the needs beyond our customary concerns. May our hands be open to give of what we have and to receive the never-ending flow of blessings from our very creative God. May we learn, from God's creativity, endless ways to stretch and multiply our resources so that the greatest needs will always be served.

Let us take a moment in silence to remember the times when God provided.

Pause.

> With renewed trust, let us commit ourselves to shepherd the resources given to us.

All: Lord God, giver of all good gifts, we humbly acknowledge that everything we have comes from you. We are entrusted with the material goods of this parish community and so we ask that you give us wisdom and compassion in directing their use. Mindful of the words of Tobit to his son and the instructions of the apostles to the Christians in Jerusalem, we will not turn away from the needy. Mindful of Jesus' encouraging words, we will not worry about our own needs. We strive first for your kingdom, God, believing in your abundance.

Closing Song: "We Will Serve the Lord" by Rory Cooney (OCP)

Prayer to Recognize Our Calling

Suggestion for use: This prayer is appropriate for a vocation conference or a youth retreat. It could also be used at the gathering of any organization in the parish, especially when members are seeking how to be of service or are celebrating new membership.

Opening Song: "Cry the Gospel" by Tom Booth (OCP)

Leader: Though we know our baptism calls us to proclaim the gospel, to spread God's love, to show concern for the poor and to bring healing to our world, sometimes we resist the persistent, personal call through which God summons us for a specific work. In this, we are not alone. The Scriptures give us numerous examples of God's call and people's initial resistance or doubt about their ability to do what God is asking.

First Reader: The Call of Moses, the Liberator; Exodus 3:1–7, 10; 4:10–13

Second Reader: The Call of Gideon, a Judge; Judges 6: 11-16

First Reader: The Call of Jeremiah, a Prophet; Jeremiah 1:4–8

Second Reader: The Call of Mary, Mother of Jesus; Luke 1:26 35

Leader: Notice that with every expression of doubt or hesitancy, God gives assurances that the person will not act alone. If God asks someone to do something, God also provides assistance so the work can be accomplished. A call from God can be frightening. But comfort and peace accompany the request. Let us pray for courage to respond when God calls us.

All: Lord, giver of gifts and author of souls, you know what is needed in our world and you know how each of us can help to build your kingdom. Give us courage to take on the work that needs to be done. Give us faith that you are working by our side. Give us confidence to accomplish good things in your name. Amen.

Song: "Pescador de Hombres (Lord, You Have Come)" (verses 1 and 2) by Cesareo Gabarain (OCP)

First Reader: 1 Corinthians 1:26–31

Leader: God, you created us with gifts and talents for a purpose,
All: Let us hear you when you call.

Leader: God, you placed a generous heart within each of us,
All: Let us hear you when you call.

Leader: God, you gave us dreams and the breath of life,
All: Let us hear you when you call.

Leader: Jesus, you saw potential in the people attracted to your message,
All: Let us hear you when you call.

Leader: Jesus, you chose diverse people to carry on your work,

All: Let us hear you when you call.

Leader: Jesus, you felt the sincerity of those who wanted to serve,
All: Let us hear you when you call.

Leader: Spirit of God, you re-create shattered dreams and renew sagging spirits,
All: Let us hear you when you call.

Leader: Spirit of God, you inspire direction and purpose,
All: Let us hear you when you call.

Leader: Spirit of God, you anoint believers for the work of the kingdom,
All: Let us hear you when you call.

Second Reader: John 15:15–16

All: God who called us into being and who has great plans for us, we ask you for the grace to know our purpose in its ever-changing forms. Called by baptism to love and serve, we seek to be faithful to our vocation. In our chosen lifestyles and through our ministries of service, may we honor the process of coming to know, love and serve you better every day of our lives. Amen.

Song: "Pescador de Hombres (Lord, You Have Come)" (verses 3, 4) by Cesareo Gabarain (OCP)

Prayer for World Peace

Suggestion for use: This prayer is appropriate for times of war, when our nation or any nation is in crisis, or any time the parish community wants to focus its concern on the need for people everywhere to heal relationships and grow in tolerance.

Opening Song: "Let There Be Peace on Earth" by Sy Miller and Jill Jackson (Jan-Lee Music)

Leader: Our world needs peace, and God desires this peace for all people. Each of us, by joining our desire to the heart of God, can find within ourselves a way to do our own small part in the peacemaking effort. At this time, we come together to look at the larger picture of nations joining hands in peace. With this vision, a dream shared by prophets before us, we hope to carry the intention of peace always.

First Reader: Micah 4:1–5

Response: Psalm 122

Side 1: I was glad when they said to me, "Let us go to the house of the Lord!" Our feet are standing within your gates, O Jerusalem.
Side 2: Jerusalem—built as a city that is bound firmly together. To it the tribes go up, the tribes of the Lord, as was decreed for Israel, to give thanks to the name of the Lord.

Side 1: For there the thrones for judgment were set up, the thrones of the house of David.
Side 2: Pray for the peace of Jerusalem; "May they prosper who love you. Peace be within your walls, and security within your towers."

Side 1: For the sake of my relatives and friends I will say, "Peace be within you."
Side 2: For the sake of the house of the Lord our God, I will seek your good.

Leader: The vision of many nations coming together seeking peace, as we heard it from the prophet Micah, had its modern fulfillment in 1986 when Pope John Paul II invited the leaders of major world religions to come together to pray for peace. Just as Psalm 122 celebrates many tribes together ascending the holy mountain in Jerusalem, so too the 1986 peace-seekers climbed the Umbrian hills into Assisi, the hometown of the peacemaker, Saint Francis. Here, representing their various religions, the leaders did something remarkable.

James Twyman, the modern-day troubadour who gives peace concerts around the world, describes this gathering of religious leaders in his book, *Praying Peace*. He says,

In a ceremony that may prove to be of monumental importance in the centuries to come, each one of these spiritual masters prayed the prayer from their tradition that defined their own longing for peace. They prayed and they listened, and when all was said and done, there was one important realization—they all wanted the same thing. More than that, if you took certain definitive words like Allah, Buddha or Christ out of the prayers, it was hard to tell which prayer belonged to which religion. How brilliant! The world began to realize that we aren't so far apart after all. And the religions of the world, those very institutions that had often used faith in a loving God as the launch pad for intolerance and war, became the bright beacons that would initiate a new era of peace.[7]

All: Lord, it helps to know we are not alone in our desire for peace. Good people everywhere in the world are seeking right relationships, just solutions, spiritual awakening, resolution of conflict. We join our prayer with our human family around the world. Come, Prince of Peace, and heal what is torn.

Leader: Let us take a silent moment to think of some area in our personal lives where peace is lacking. In the silence, invite Christ to bring peace to that situation. Be aware that Christ may also bring a challenge—something that will be required of us so peace can happen.

Pause.

Second Reader: Peace I leave with you; my peace I give to you. I do not give to you as the world gives. Do not let your hearts be troubled, and do not let them be afraid.

All: But now in Christ Jesus you who once were far off have been brought near by the blood of Christ. For he is our peace; in his flesh he has made both groups into one and has broken down the dividing wall, that is, the hostility between us.

Leader: Peace I leave with you; my peace I give to

you. I do not give to you as the world gives. Do not let your hearts be troubled, and do not let them be afraid.

All: He has abolished the law with its commandments and ordinances, that he might create in himself one new humanity in place of the two, thus making peace, and might reconcile both groups to God in one body through the cross, thus putting to death that hostility through it.

Leader: Peace I leave with you; my peace I give to you. I do not give to you as the world gives. Do not let your hearts be troubled, and do not let them be afraid.

All: So he came and proclaimed peace to you who were far off and peace to those who were near; for through him both of us have access in one spirit to the Father.

Leader: Peace I leave with you; my peace I give to you. I do not give to you as the world gives. Do not let your hearts be troubled, and do not let them be afraid.

All: So then you are no longer strangers and aliens, but you are citizens with the saints and also members of the household of God, built upon the foundation of the apostles and prophets, with Christ Jesus himself as the cornerstone.

Leader: Peace I leave with you; my peace I give to you. I do not give to you as the world gives. Do not let your hearts be troubled, and do not let them be afraid.

All: In him the whole structure is joined together and grows into a holy temple in the Lord; in whom you also are built together spiritually into a dwelling place for God.

Leader: Peace I leave with you; my peace I give to you. I do not give to you as the world gives. Do not let your hearts be troubled, and do not let them be afraid.

All: Amen.

Closing Song: "This Is My Song" (Lorenz)

Prayer in Times of Special Need

Suggestion for use: This is a prayer of pure longing. When God is sorely needed, whatever the reason, use this prayer with the parish community or any group. Provide paper and pencils for the written activity described below.

Opening: Begin in quiet, after all are assembled. Play the meditation song, "So Longs My, Soul" by Liam Lawton from the album *In the Quiet* (GIA). If music is available to group members, invite them to sing along.

Leader: We gather here, in this time of special need, to ask God to be among us in our conscious awareness. We know that without God we can do nothing, but with God nothing is impossible.

Reader: Romans 8:28–30

All: We know that all things work together for good for those who love God.

Leader: Sometimes, when difficulties confront us, we aren't even sure we know who God is. The God we thought we knew eludes us, and we begin to doubt what we had believed. Let us think about the God we envision. First, we will hear some possible ways to complete the phrase "God is… ". Then you will have time to write your own description.

Reader: (*Read slowly, pausing after each description.*)

God is what I feel when I'm singing!
God is more than good: God *is* the Good!
Good overcomes evil, triumphs over wickedness, renews hope, has the power to change hearts. That's God.
God is energy universal and infused, enfolding and empowering.
God is present within each person, finding expression through the feminine gifts of each woman and the masculine gifts of each man.
Because God's energy pervades the universe, hands extended to touch can heal, hearts raised in prayer can direct a course of events.
God is the Love that creates unity, harmony, joy, peace, forgiveness. When love is invited in, God can't be absent. When one refuses to love, God can't be present.
God is in the seasons and the patterns and the progress of enlightenment. God has always been God. It is I whose understanding changes.
God is what I perceive when I am growing!
God is ultimate reality, the source of all that is. Moment by moment we create our own destiny as we choose to or refuse to cooperate with the energy force for good that supports our existence.
God is and I have a whole lifetime, extending even beyond time, to discover what that means.

Pause.

Leader: Using the paper provided, make your own list of who God is.

Allow time for writing. Sharing with one other person or in a small group is an optional follow-up to the writing. After the writing (and sharing), leader calls the group to prayer.

Response: Psalm 62:1–2, 5–8, 11–12

Leader: God, however we envision God, is ultimately Love. This is why we need God, and so we pray:

Side 1: For God alone my soul waits in silence; from him comes my salvation. He alone is my rock and my salvation, my fortress; I shall never be shaken.

Side 2: For God alone my soul waits in silence, for my hope is from him. He alone is my rock and my salvation, my fortress; I shall not be shaken.

Side 1: On God rests my deliverance and my honor; my mighty rock, my refuge is in God.

Side 2: Trust in him at all times, O people; pour out your heart before him; God is a refuge for us.

Side 1: Once God has spoken; twice have I heard this: that power belongs to God.

Side 2: Steadfast love belongs to you, O Lord. For you repay to all according to their work.

Closing Song: "Seek Ye First" by Karen Lafferty (Maranatha! Music)

NOTES

1 Margaret Alter, *Resurrection Psychology* (Chicago: Loyola, 1994), pp. 169, 170.

2 Virginia Smith, *God for Grownups* (Allen, Tex.: Thomas More, 2002), pp. 76, 77.

3 Murray Bodo, *Tales of Saint Francis* (Cincinnati: St. Anthony Messenger Press, 1992) pp. 180, 181.

4 John Kirvan, *God Hunger* (Notre Dame, Ind.: Sorin Books, 1999) p. 48.

5 Robert J. Wicks, *After 50: Spiritually Embracing Your Own Wisdom Years* (Mahwah, N.J.: Paulist, 1997), pp. 37, 38.

6 Joan Chittister, *The Fire in These Ashes* (Lanham, Md.: Sheed and Ward, 1995), pp. 84, 85.

7 James F. Twyman, *Praying Peace* (Findhorn, U.K.: Findhorn Press, 2000), pp. 17, 18.